The Spirit of the Lord God

The Spirit of the Lord God

Biblical Names and Images for the Holy Spirit;
An Abecedarian Anthology of Spiritual Reflections
for Anytime

The **Spirit** of the **Lord God**

MARK G. BOYER

RESOURCE *Publications* · Eugene, Oregon

THE SPIRIT OF THE LORD GOD
Biblical Names and Images for the Holy Spirit; An Abecedarian Anthology of
Spiritual Reflections for Anytime

Resource Publications
An Imprint of Wipf and Stock Publishers
199 W. 8th Ave., Suite 3
Eugene, OR 97401

www.wipfandstock.com

PAPERBACK ISBN: 979-8-3852-2384-8
HARDCOVER ISBN: 979-8-3852-2385-5
EBOOK ISBN: 979-8-3852-2386-2

07/03/24

Not by might, nor by power, but by my spirit, say the LORD of hosts.

—Zech 4:6

Spirit of the Universe,

O Eternal Light of Lights,

Spirit of the Universe,

we bow to you.

Most Holy and Boundless

Breath of Creation,

forever and ever

we bow to you.

—Shantivanam Retreat Center

Contents

CONTENTS

F

G

H

I

J

K

L

Contents

Contents

Abbreviations

BCE = Before the Common Era (same as BC = Before Christ)

CB (NT) = Christian Bible (New Testament)
    Acts = Acts of the Apostles
    Col = Letter to the Colossians
    1 Cor = First Letter of Paul to the Corinthians
    2 Cor = Second Letter of Paul to the Corinthians
    Eph = Letter to the Ephesians
    Gal = Letter of Paul to the Galatians
    Heb = Letter to the Hebrews
    Jas = Letter of James
    John = John's Gospel
    1 John = First Letter of John
    Jude = Letter of Jude
    Luke = Luke's Gospel
    Mark = Mark's Gospel
    Matt = Matthew's Gospel
    1 Pet = First Letter of Peter
    2 Pet = Second Letter of Peter
    Phil = Letter of Paul to the Philippians
    Rev = Revelation
    Rom = Letter of Paul to the Romans
    1 Thess = First Letter of Paul to the Thessalonians
    2 Thess = Second Letter to the Thessalonians
    2 Tim = Second Letter to Timothy
    Titus = Letter to Titus

CE = Common Era (same as AD = *Anno Domini*, in the year of the Lord)

HB (OT) = Hebrew Bible (Old Testament)
Amos = Amos
1 Chr = First Book of Chronicles
2 Chr = Second Book of Chronicles
Dan = Daniel
Deut = Deuteronomy
Eccl = Ecclesiastes
Exod = Exodus
Ezra = Ezra
Ezek = Ezekiel
Gen = Genesis
Hag = Haggai
Hos = Hosea
Isa = Isaiah
Jer = Jeremiah
Job = Job
Joel = Joel
Judg = Judges
1 Kgs = First Book of Kings
2 Kgs = Second Book of Kings
Lam = Lamentations
Lev = Leviticus
Mal = Malachi
Mic = Micah
Nah = Nahum
Num = Numbers
Prov = Proverbs
Ps(s) = Psalm(s)
1 Sam = First Book of Samuel
2 Sam = Second Book of Samuel
Song = Song of Songs
Zech = Zechariah
Zeph = Zephaniah

NRSV = New Revised Standard Version

OT (A) = Old Testament (Apocrypha)
Bar = Baruch
1 Esd = First Book of Esdras

2 Esd = Second Book of Esdras
Jdt = Judith
2 Macc = Second Book of Maccabees
3 Macc = Third Book of Maccabees
4 Macc = Fourth Book of Maccabees
Sir = Sirach (Ecclesiasticus)
Sus = Susanna
Wis = Wisdom (of Solomon)

Peterson = *The Message*

Punctuation Usage

/ = indicates where one line of poetic text ends and another begins

(biblical notation) = see the specific biblical verse(s) in parentheses for more information

– = range of verses following a colon (8:3–4)

— = range of verses from a verse in one chapter to a verse in another chapter (8:3—9:4)

a, b, c = designates first (a), second (b), third (c), etc. sentence in a verse of Scripture or a line of poetic text

Introduction

The $\mathfrak{Spirit}$ of the $\mathfrak{Lord}$ $\mathfrak{God}$

The Spirit

The Spirit, a biblical term for the invisible power and life-source of God, is found in the Hebrew Bible (Old Testament), Old Testament (Apocrypha), and the Christian Bible (New Testament). All the entries in this book begin with biblical passages. The Scriptures have been selected from a variety of biblical material that mentions the Spirit of the Lord, the Spirit of the Lord God, the Holy Spirit, the Spirit, etc.

of the Lord God

Lord God refers to the God of the Hebrews, Israelites, and Jews in the HB (OT) and the Old Testament (Apocrypha). The Spirit of the Lord, the Spirit of God, the Holy Spirit, or, simply, the Spirit in the CB (NT) refers to that life-giving power of God that raised his Son, Jesus, from the dead. It is important not to reach a conclusion about the doctrine of the Trinity when reviewing biblical material about the Spirit of the Lord God, because the doctrine of the Trinity did not develop until after the Bible had been written.

A name is a word, term, or phrase by which somebody or something is known and distinguished from other people or things. In the Bible there are different names used to identify the Spirit along with images that explain what the Spirit is like. The seventy-three entries in this book are not exhaustive; they are representative of the names for and the images of the Holy Spirit.

SUBTITLES: *BIBLICAL NAMES AND IMAGES FOR THE HOLY SPIRIT, AN ABECEDARIAN ANTHOLOGY OF SPIRITUAL REFLECTIONS FOR ANYTIME*

Biblical Names and Images for the Holy Spirit

In the Bible, there are not many biblical names for the Holy Spirit. The few that exist are found in the pages that follow. There are more images—metaphors, comparisons, similes—than there are names. The reason for this fact is that the Hebrew word for spirit—*ruah*—and the Greek word for spirit—*pneuma*—can mean breath, wind, or spirit. This makes it difficult to capture a description of the Spirit in words or even to imagine a picture of breath, wind, or spirit.

Ancient people experienced an invisible, life-producing force named breath, which when present indicated life, and when absent, indicated death. Like that force named breath was the force named wind, which could be heard and felt, but could not be seen. Ancient people concluded that their experiences of breath and wind must be experiences of their God named Yahweh (LORD). Thus, just like people breathed, so God breathed; in English, we call God's breath Spirit. While we have a separate name for Spirit, Hebrew and Greek had only *ruah* and *pneuma* for breath, wind, and spirit. At the beginning of the HB (OT) book of Genesis, the author presents God as a mighty wind sweeping over the waters of chaos and as blowing the breath of life into his creation. In English, we would say that he inspirited everything he created. The author of John's Gospel presents Jesus declaring, ". . . [T]he Father has life in himself, so he has granted the Son also to have life in himself" (John 5:26). The life that the Father has in himself and which he shared with his Son, so the Son has life in himself, is the Spirit. Trying to describe that life (Spirit) is like the smoke formation of animals in the sky in a series—A Hidden World—of porcelain plates by D. L. "Rusty" Rust, created in 1994 by The Bradford Exchange. The Finnish word for steam—*loyly* (low-loo)—found in a sauna, also means spirit; in other words, steam is like Spirit. While attempting to narrate one of Jesus' experiences of Spirit, the author of Mark's Gospel states that Jesus "sighed deeply in his spirit" (Mark 8:12), signifying the typical deep inhalation of the wonder-worker or prophet of Jesus' day before performing a mighty deed or making an authoritative utterance. In other words, the sound (sighing) indicates possession by the Spirit. More names for and images of the Spirit fill the pages that follow.

An Abecedarian

An abecedarian can refer to somebody who is learning the basics of a subject. The word can also refer to the book containing the alphabet. In other words, an abecedarian is a book, whose entries are in alphabetical order. The entries in this book begin with A and end with Z. While the English alphabet is composed of twenty-six letters, there are many entries beginning with the same letter for some names and images.

Anthology

An anthology is a printed collection of biblical names for and images of the Spirit. Each entry in the anthology consists of a name, a biblical Scripture passage, a reflection, questions for meditating and/or journaling, and a biblical psalm response.

Spiritual Reflections

A spiritual reflection is the author's exposition of the Scripture text in which the name for or the image of the Spirit occurs. The spiritual reflection is an exercise in spirituality, the method one chooses to nourish his or her spirit. The practices of spirituality are as varied as the people living on the earth. In this book, biblical passages with reflections, questions for meditation and/or journaling, and psalm responses are designed to nourish spirituality through the use of some of the biblical names for and images of the Spirit. This author has written about spirituality extensively in other books; the reader can find a list of those at the back of this book.

When reading the Bible, readers must place themselves in each book's author's time, rather than presume the readers' time. Presuming the standards of modern time, when reading a biblical book or a passage from a biblical book ignores the total context of the passage and the book. Removing the context gives Bible readers the opportunity to make any text mean whatever they want it to mean; removing the context often deprives readers of the deeper meaning of a biblical text. It is also important to recognize that an English-speaking reader is reading a translation of Hebrew, Aramaic, and Greek, and words in one language do not have a literary equivalent in another language. What is very specific in one language (like breath in English) is ambiguous in another language (like breath, wind, spirit in Hebrew [*ruah*] and Greek [*pneuma*]).

This book is based on the root word of spirituality: spirit. In the twentieth-first century, each person must be the keeper of his or her own flame of spirituality. The spiritual world gives reality to the ordinary world we experience. In his own time and place, Jesus of Nazareth used parables of the natural world as images for the spirituality of all things. The revelation of God takes place through our connection to all things Spirit. Using Native American spirituality, we can say that the Great Spirit (Wakan Tanka) is the energy (life) that flows through everything and everyone. This author's contention is that the Divine Spirit seeks to connect to the human spirit so that we have access in one Spirit to the Father (Eph 2:18).

for Anytime

The entries in this book can be used to enhance one's spirituality anytime. In other words, this is not a book to be used only during a specific liturgical season (like Christmas or Easter) or an annual season (like Spring or Summer). A person may read an entry and enhance his or her spirituality whenever he or she desires or whenever he or she deems it appropriate.

Using This Book

This book is designed to be used by individuals for private prayer. The goal of this book is to foster spirituality using names for and images of Spirit that flow from the Bible. A five-part exercise is offered for all seventy-three entries devoted to names for and images of Spirit.

1. **Title**: A short title is given to the entry. The title indicates a biblical name for or an image of the Spirit. Not only does the title give focus to the entry, but it imitates *Lectio Divina* (Divine Reading), the practice of reading a biblical passage and choosing a word or two from it for reflection, meditation, and prayer. The title is designed to promote mindfulness, the practice of maintaining a moment-by-moment awareness of thoughts, feelings, the body, and the surrounding environment. Mindfulness is the opposite of multitasking. Mindfulness is truly listening, fully tasting, deeply experiencing.

2. **Scripture**: Since the focus of the entry is found in the title, a verse or two from a Scripture passage—taken from the *New Revised Standard Version* of the Bible—illustrating the biblical source of the entry is provided.

3. **Reflection**: The Scripture passage is followed by a reflection on the biblical passage and its application to the name for or image of Spirit. Throughout the reflections, the masculine pronoun for God, LORD, LORD God, etc. is used. The author is well aware that God is neither male nor female, but in order to avoid the repetition of proper nouns over and over again, he employs male pronouns, as they are also used in most biblical translations.

4. **Meditation/Journal**: The Reflection is followed by questions for personal meditation and/or journaling. The questions function as a guide for personal appropriation of the reflection, thus leading the reader into personal prayer and/or journaling. The meditation/journal questions are designed to foster a process of actively applying the reflection to one's life, (re)interpreting an event in one's life, and further development of it. The question gets one started; where the meditation/journal goes cannot be predetermined. It may be a single statement or an idea with which one lingers for a few minutes, a few hours, or a few days. Such contemplation has no end; the reader decides when he or she has finished his or her exploration because he or she needs to attend to other things. People who like to journal—written or electronic—will find the questions appropriate for that activity.

5. **Psalm Response**: A part of a biblical psalm—taken from *The Message*—is chosen to serve as a response to the exercise. Something in the psalm may spark further prayer.

Through this process of prayer with the focus on spirituality, the reader will come to a deeper knowledge of and a closer relationship with the Spirit. Each person has a spirit, which to some degree shapes or forms his or her spirituality. The Spirit has many names and images, which, as we experience and reflect upon them, can enhance our spirituality.

NOTES ON THE BIBLE

Three Parts

The Bible is divided into two parts: The Hebrew Bible (Old Testament) and the Christian Bible (New Testament). The Hebrew Bible consists of thirty-nine named books accepted by Jews and Protestants as Holy Scripture. The Old Testament also contains those thirty-nine books plus seven to fifteen more named books or parts of books called the Apocrypha or the Deutero-canonical Books; the Old Testament is accepted by Catholics and several other Christian denominations as Holy Scripture. The Christian Bible, consisting of twenty-seven named books, is also called the New Testament; it is accepted by Christians as Holy Scripture. Thus, in this work:

— **Hebrew Bible (Old Testament)**, abbreviated **HB (OT)**, indicates that a book is found both in the Hebrew Bible and the Old Testament;

— **Old Testament (Apocrypha)**, abbreviated **OT (A)**, indicates that a book is found only in the Old Testament Apocrypha and not in the Hebrew Bible;

— and **Christian Bible (New Testament)**, abbreviated **CB (NT)**, indicates that a book is found only in the Christian Bible or New Testament.

In notating biblical texts, the first number refers to the chapter in the book, and the second number (following the colon) refers to the verse within the chapter. Thus, HB (OT) Isa 7:11 means that the quotation comes from Isaiah, chapter 7, verse 11. OT (A) Sir 39:30 means that the quotation comes from Sirach, chapter 39, verse 30. CB (NT) Mark 6:2 means that the quotation comes from Mark's Gospel, chapter 6, verse 2. When more than one sentence appears in a verse, the letters a, b, c, etc. indicate the sentence being referenced in the verse. Thus, HB (OT) 2 Kgs 1:6a means that the quotation comes from the Second Book of Kings, chapter 1, verse 6, sentence 1. Also, poetry, such as the Psalms and sections of Judith, Proverbs, Isaiah, and others may be noted using the letters a, b, c, etc. to indicate the lines being used. Thus, Ps 16:4a refers to the first line of verse 4 of Psalm 16; there are two more lines of verse 4: b and c.

Because there may be a difference in the verse numbers between the *New Revised Standard Version* (NRSV) and the Vulgate (the Latin translation of the Septuagint, such as *The New American Bible Revised Edition* [NABRE]), alternative verse numbers appear in parentheses or brackets as necessary. This is true particularly with the Psalms, but with other books as well. Thus, NRSV Isaiah 9:2–7 is NABRE (Vulgate) Isaiah 9:1–6; NRSV Isaiah 9:2–4, 6–7 is NABRE (Vulgate) Isaiah 9:1–3, 5–6. Introductory material to Bibles usually indicates which verse-numbering is being used.

In the HB (OT) and the OT (A), the reader often sees LORD (note all capital letters). Because God's name (Yahweh or YHWH, referred to as the Tetragrammaton) is not to be pronounced, the name Adonai (meaning *Lord*) is substituted for Yahweh when a biblical text is read. When a biblical text is translated and printed, LORD (Gen 2:4) is used to alert the reader to what the text actually states: Yahweh. Furthermore, when the biblical author writes Lord Yahweh, printers present Lord GOD (note all capital letters for GOD; Gen 15:2) to avoid the printed ambiguity of LORD LORD. The Psalms in *The Message*, substitutes GOD (note all capital letters) for Yahweh. When the reference is to Jesus, the word printed is Lord (note capital L and lower-case letters; Luke 11:1). When writing about a lord (note all lower-case letters; Matt 18:25) with servants, no capital L is used.

In this book, *cf* (meaning *confer*) has not been used. Biblical notations placed in parentheses indicate where the reference can be found in the Bible. For example, the Second Book of Samuel records King David writing a song (2 Sam 22:1–51). The notation in parentheses is given to the reader, who may wish to look up the full reference in his or her Bible. In some instances, a number of notations appear in parentheses; again, the reader may wish to see the references in their contexts.

Bibles

Most Bible readers are not aware that there is no such thing as the original Bible! The fact is: There are Bibles. First, there is the Jewish Bible, often called the Hebrew Bible; its books were collected and completed between 70 and 90 CE based on the Jerusalem canon (collection) in this order: Torah (Genesis, Exodus, Leviticus, Numbers, Deuteronomy), Prophets (Isaiah, Jeremiah, Ezekiel, etc.), and Writings (Job, Psalms, Proverbs, etc). It is important to note the arrangement of the collected books. Second, there is—for want of a better name—the Christian Hebrew Bible, completed in the fourth century CE, but not defined until after the Reformation. It consists of Torah, Writings, and Prophets. It is important to note the (re)ordering of the collected books. Christianity took the Jewish (Hebrew) Bible and rearranged the order of its books! Then, Christianity named it the Old Testament.

The Jerusalem canon, obviously, is the collection of biblical books used in Jerusalem and its environs. A large community of Jews, however, lived in Alexandria, Egypt. To the Jerusalem canon (books in Hebrew and Aramaic) they added books in Greek, the language they spoke; this collection is the Alexandrine canon. They also translated the Jerusalem canon's books from Hebrew and Aramaic into Greek. That translation, containing books and parts of books not in the Jerusalem canon, is called the Septuagint (abbreviated LXX). Later, the Septuagint was translated into Latin; it is known as the Vulgate. Every time a book of the Bible is translated, it picks up something and it loses something; that is because there is no such thing as literary equivalence.

Thus, we have (1) the Hebrew Bible—the Jewish Bible, (2) the Hebrew Bible (Old Testament)—the rearranged books of the Hebrew Bible, and (3) the Christian Bible—twenty-seven books originally written in Greek. The Protestant Bible contains only the books in the Jerusalem canon, but rearranged into the Old Testament, plus the Christian Bible books; the Catholic Bible contains the books in the Alexandrine collection plus the Christian Bible books.

The extra books or parts of books found in the Catholic Bible (and coming from the Alexandrine collection of the Jewish Bible), but not found in a Protestant Bible, are collectively referred to as the Apocrypha or Deuterocanonical Books. They include Tobit, Judith, additions to Esther, Wisdom of Solomon, Sirach (Ecclesiasticus), Baruch, Letter of Jeremiah, Prayer of Azariah (addition to Daniel), Susanna (addition to Daniel), Bel and the Dragon (addition to Daniel), 1 Maccabees, 2 Maccabees, 1 Esdras, Prayer of Manasseh, Psalm 151, 3 Maccabees, 2 Esdras, and 4 Maccabees. Not every Christian group, such as Catholics, accepts all the books in the Apocrypha as Scripture; for example, out of the four books of Maccabees, Catholics accept only 1 and 2 Maccabees. In Catholic Bibles, the additional books are placed with similar books. Thus, First and Second Maccabees are inserted with the historical books; the books of Wisdom and Sirach are found in the wisdom literature section.

Thus, there is no single or original Bible; there are many Bibles; it depends on what books a specific denomination or group (Jews, Christians) accepts as Scripture. The Bible that contains any book that any group accepts as Scripture is *The Access Bible* (updated edition): *New Revised Standard Version with the Apocrypha*, general editors Gail R. O'Day and David Petersen, published in New York by Oxford University Press in 1999 and updated in 2011. This book uses *The Access Bible* for all Scriptures and Reflections. This book also uses *The Message: Catholic/Ecumenical Edition, The Bible in Contemporary Language* by Eugene H. Peterson, published by ACTA Publications, Chicago, 2013, for all Psalm Responses.

Thus, a Bible reader should keep in mind the following: In a Christian Bible, The Old Testament consists of the rearranged books found in the Hebrew (Jewish) Bible. Roman Catholics and some others add some books and parts of books to that Old Testament because they were found in the Alexandrine collection. In general, Protestants do not add books to the Old Testament; they follow the Jerusalem collection of books, but rearrange them as noted above. Almost all Christians accept the twenty-seven books of the New Testament; there are a few groups that reject one or another of the books in the collection.

Thus, as you can see, this can become difficult to navigate, especially when someone says, "The Bible says . . . ." The astute Bible reader needs to ask, "Which book in which Bible says that?" There is no such thing as the original Bible. There are Bibles, various libraries of books collected over three thousand years by individuals and groups who declared their collection (canon) to be Scripture. When engaged in Bible study, it is also important to note that the Bible is a library of books written by different authors at different times in history; it is not a single book.

Presuppositions

The HB (OT) begins as stories passed on by word of mouth from one person to another. Sometime during the oral transmission stage, authors decided to collect the oral stories and write them. A change occurs immediately. One does not tell a story the same way one writes a story. Repetition and correction occur in oral story-telling. Except for future emendations by copyists, single statements by characters and plot structure dominate written stories. Furthermore, in both oral and written story-telling, types or models are employed. In the HB (OT), for example, Joshua and Elijah are types of Moses. In the CB (NT) Elizabeth becomes a type of Hannah, who is herself a type of Sarah. When orally narrating or writing a story, the teller or author consciously creates one character as a type of another in order to make the character and his or her words and actions intelligible to the hearer or reader.

In the CB (NT) the oldest gospel is Mark's account of Jesus' victory. The author of Matthew's Gospel copied and shortened about eighty percent of Mark's material into his book and then added other stories to make the work longer. The author of Luke's Gospel copied and shortened about fifty percent of Mark's material into his orderly account and then added other stories to make the work much longer. The material shared by Matthew and Luke is called Q—from the German word *Quelle*, meaning *Source*—by biblical scholars. Mark's Gospel begins as oral story-telling, lasting for about forty years in that form. An unidentified author, called Mark for the sake of convenience, collects the oral stories, sets a plot, and writes the first gospel around 70 CE. Because Jesus was expected to return soon, no one had thought about recording what he had said and done until Mark came along and realized that he was not returning as quickly as had been thought. About ten years after Mark finished his gospel, Matthew needed to adopt Mark's narrative—originally intended for a peasant Gentile readership—to a Jewish audience. And about twenty years after Mark finished his gospel, Luke needed to adapt Mark's poor Gentile-intended work for a rich, upper class, urban, Gentile readership. The author of John's Gospel did not know the existence of the other three works collectively named synoptic gospels. A point often overlooked by modern readers is the fact that they are not the intended readers of biblical texts. Every biblical book was written to a specific group of people at a specific time in history. Thus, Paul did not write to people living in the United States; he wrote in Greek to people living in Rome, Corinth, and Thessalonica. Modern readers are reading an English translation (and interpretation) with Roman-Greco cultural presuppositions underlying the text.

Furthermore, letters and gospels were not first intended to be read privately as is done today. They were meant to be heard in a group. The very low rate of literacy in the first century would have never dictated many copies of texts since most people could not read, and their standard practice was to listen to another read the letters and stories to them. Thus, what began as oral story-telling passed on by word of mouth became written story-telling preserved in gospels. A careful reading of Mark's Gospel will reveal the orality still embedded in the text, especially evident in the repetition of words and the organization of stories in three parts. In rewriting Mark, Matthew and Luke remove the last traces of oral story-telling.

The letters of Paul are older than the gospels. Biblical scholars divide the letters of Paul into the authentic letters—those written by Paul (Romans, Galatians, Philippians, etc.)—and those written by someone else in Paul's name—second generation Pauline letters (Ephesians, Colossians, Titus, etc.). The latter group of letters usually develop Pauline thought for a new generation of Christians. The reader of letters needs to keep in mind that the letter was not addressed to him or her; it was addressed to a specific group of believers in the mid- to late-first century CE. In addition to the Pauline body of letters, there are other letters that were gathered and placed in the CB (NT) canon (collection), such as James, 1 and 2 Peter, Jude, etc. These anonymous letters were written in the name of an apostle to give them authority in the Christian communities to which they were addressed.

The Spirit of the Lord God

A

Abide

Scripture: ". . . [T]he LORD said, 'My spirit shall not abide in mortals forever, for they are flesh; their days shall be one hundred twenty years.'" (Gen 6:3)

Reflection: Based on the portrayal of God as a potter making people out of clay (Gen 2:7) and breathing his spirit into what he created (Gen 2:7), according to the mythology of the HB (OT) book of Genesis, God decides to limit the length of human years to one hundred twenty. That number of human years is a multiple of forty, a sacred biblical number, referring to the life of an average human generation, a long period of trial, a long time. When forty is multiplied by three, another sacred number referring to the divine, grace, gift, the total is one hundred twenty, indicating a long, abundant life. So, rather than understanding a lifetime of God's spirit abiding in mortals for a limited time, it is better to grasp that one hundred twenty years is the blessing of an abundance of a lifetime. "My spirit abides among you," says the LORD, as recorded by the prophet Haggai (2:5b).

While it is the Johannine Jesus, who is best known for his abide language (John 6:56; 14:17; 15:4–10), Paul expresses the same idea in his CB (NT) letter to the Romans. He tells them to live according to the Spirit (Rom 8:5, 13). Other images include walking according to the Spirit (Rom 8:4) and setting one's mind on the things of the Spirit (Rom 8:5–6). Indirectly referencing the abide language of Genesis, Paul tells the Romans that they "are in the Spirit, since the Spirit of God dwells" in them (Rom 8:9).

1

Meditation/Journal: What is the average lifespan of people in your family? Of how many years do you consider a long abundant lifetime to consist? In what specific ways do you experience the Spirit abiding in you?

Psalm Response: "You who sit down in the High God's presence, / spend the night in Shaddai's shadow, / Say this, 'GOD, you're my refuge. / I trust in you and I'm safe!' / His huge outstretched arms protect you— / under them you're perfectly safe; / his arms fend off all harm." (Ps 91:1–2, 4)

Spirit of Adoption

Scripture: ". . . [Y]ou did not receive a spirit of slavery . . . , but you have received a spirit of adoption." (Rom 8:15)

Reflection: The word *adoption* means *to raise someone's child as one's own*. In his letter to the Romans, Paul tells his readers that the spirit they have received is not one characterized by the master-slave image; God is not a master, and they are not slaves. Rather, they are adopted children. Through their faith that God raised Jesus from the dead, they have "the first fruits of the Spirit" and they "groan inwardly while [they] wait for adoption, the redemption of [their] bodies" (Rom 8:23). The first fruits is an image taken from the harvest; what was harvested first indicated what was to come. Likewise, the spirit of adoption is a foretaste of future glory. In his letter to the Galatians, Paul uses the master-slave image, writing, "God has sent the Spirit of his Son into our hearts . . . . So you are no longer a slave . . ." (Gal 4:6–7). The result of God's sending of his Son is adoption, which results in reception of the Spirit, who raised Jesus from the dead. Thus, the experience of the Spirit is an experience of the Risen Christ.

The Spirit of adoption enables believers to cry "Abba! Father!" (Rom 8:15; Gal 4:6). Paul explains that "it is that very Spirit bearing witness with our spirit" (Rom 8:16). In other words, spirit (the individual) connects to Spirit (the divine), and like others who have been adopted, we call God Father, just like Jesus did (Mark 14:36), because we are "heirs of God and joint heirs with Christ" (Rom 8:17; Gal 4:7). Through Jesus, God has adopted both Jews and Gentiles, and he has connected his Spirit to their spirits. The result of the power of God—the Spirit—is transformation of life, just like adoption transforms life, but for God it also means transformation of bodies through resurrection. The model for both transformed life and transformed body is, of course, Jesus, in Pauline understanding.

Meditation/Journal: In what ways have you experienced the Spirit of adoption? In other words, how have you experienced the Spirit connecting to your spirit? What transformation has occurred in you?

Psalm Response: "Point out the road I must travel [, God,]; / I'm all ears, all eyes before you. / Teach me how to live to please you, / because you're my God. / Lead me by your blessed Spirit / into cleared and level pastureland." (Ps 143:8b, 10)

Advocate

Scripture: Jesus said, ". . . I will ask the Father, and he will give you another Advocate to be with you forever." (John 14:16)

Reflection: Unique to the CB (NT) Gospel according to John is Jesus' statement to his followers that he will ask the Father to send them another Advocate, who is identified as the Holy Spirit (John 14:17, 26; 15:26). ". . . [I]f I do not go away," states Jesus, "the Advocate will not come to you . . . ." (John 16:7). The Greek word Paraclete, translated as Advocate, is transliterated into English as Paraclete. It means one who is called to the side of another in need of assistance in legal matters, like a lawyer, who pleads one's case. Thus, when Paraclete is translated, it often appears as Helper. In the First Letter of John, the author declares that Jesus is the advocate with the Father (1 John 2:1); this means that Jesus is the Paraclete, the Helper, who pleads (intercedes) with the Father, who sends the Spirit as another Advocate. The word *Paraclete* is used only five times in the CB (NT) (John 14:16, 26; 15:26; 16:7; and 1 John 2:1). Thus, the word can refer to Jesus' renewed presence as the Spirit or the Spirit, who takes Jesus' place.

In Johannine literature, the Advocate (Paraclete) has three tasks: He will prove the world wrong about sin, righteousness, and judgement (John 16:8); he will vindicate the righteousness of Jesus (John 16:10); and he will judge the world (John 16:11). It is important to keep in mind that this is the role of the Spirit in Johannine literature and does not appear in other biblical literature. As Advocate, the Holy Spirit supports and speaks in favor of Jesus' followers; the Holy Spirit is a helper, who acts or intercedes on behalf of Jesus' followers. He is like a lawyer, who pleads cases before the Father.

Meditation/Journal: Who has served as an Advocate (Paraclete, Helper) for you? What did he or she do for you?

Psalm Response: "God, for your sake, help me! / Use your influence to clear me. / Listen, God—I'm desperate. / Don't be too busy to hear me. / Oh, look! God's right here helping! / GOD's on my side." (Ps 54:1–2, 4)

Agape (Love)

Scripture: "I appeal to you, brothers and sisters, by our Lord Jesus Christ and by the love of the Spirit, to join me in earnest prayer to God on my behalf . . . ." (Rom 15:30)

Reflection: The Greek word used by Paul for love in the above verse from his letter to the Romans is agape. While Greek is rich in words for love—*agape, philia, storge,* and *eros*—English is poor, having only one word for love: love. Agape designates self-sacrificing love; the greater good of another is place ahead of self. Agape wills the good of another. Near the end of his letter to the Romans, Paul appeals to his readers by the love of the Spirit. Earlier in the letter he had written that "God's love has been poured into our hearts through the Holy Spirit that has been given to us" (Rom 5:5). Both Jewish and Gentile Christians share in the love of the Spirit. Thus, Paul hopes that the mutual sharing of the love of the Spirit will result in mutual prayer and support for the collection he desires to take to Jerusalem.

In the second-generation Pauline letter to the Colossians, the author states that Epaphras, a faithful minister, "has made known to us your love in the Spirit" (Col 1:8). In other words, the love among the members of the community is generated by the Spirit; self-sacrificing love from the Spirit exists among the members of the community in Colossae (Col 1:4) and, by extension, to the author of the letter. The unification accomplished by the Spirit brings all together in an invisible bond of love. It leads to prayer, donations, and deep concern for members of the community.

Meditation/Journal: To whom are you united by the love of the Spirit? Make a list. For each indicate what self-sacrificing you have done for him or her.

Psalm Response: " . . . I pray. / GOD, it's time for a break! / God, answer in love! / Answer with your sure salvation. / Now answer me, GOD, because

4

you love me; / Let me see your mercy full-face. / . . . [T]he children of his servants will get it, / The lovers of his name will live in it." (Ps 69:13, 16, 36)

𝕭

𝕭reath

Scripture: "The hand of the LORD came upon me, and he brought me out by the spirit of the LORD and set me down in the middle of a valley; it was full of bones. He said to me, 'Mortal, can these bones live?' I answered, 'O Lord GOD, you know.' Then he said to me, "[S]ay to them: O dry bones hear the word of the LORD. Thus says the Lord GOD to these bones: I will cause breath to enter you, and you shall live." I looked, and there were sinews on them, and flesh had come upon them, and skin had covered them; but there was no breath in them. Then he said to me, 'Prophesy to the breath, prophesy, mortal, and say to the breath: Thus says the Lord GOD: Come from the four winds, O breath, and breathe upon these slain that they may live.' I prophesied as he commanded me, and the breath came into them, and they lived . . . ." (Ezek 37:1, 3–4, 8–10)

Reflection: In Hebrew, the word *ruah* can mean *wind, breath,* or *spirit.* In the NRSV account of Ezekiel's vision of dry bones coming to life above, the word *ruah* carries all three of those meanings. The bones arise, but they have no breath in them; a footnote in the NRSV Bible states that the word *ruah* could be translated as wind or spirit. God tells Ezekiel to call upon the four winds (North, South, East, and West)—*ruah*— to bring breath—*ruah*—and they are filled with spirit—*ruah*—and come alive. For biblical authors and ancient people, breath is life; those who are alive breath. Those who are dead do not breathe, and neither do idols. This understanding begins with the author of the HB (OT) book of Genesis. After portraying God as a potter, forming a man from the dust of the ground, the author states that the LORD God "breathed into his nostrils the breath of life, and the man became a living being" (Gen 2:7). The author of the OT (A) book of Second Esdras notes that God "formed human beings and put a heart in the midst of each body, and gave each person breath and life and understanding and the spirit of Almighty God" (2 Esd 16:61–62). A footnote in the NRSV

Bible states that the word *spirit* could also be translated as *breath*! Those who are dead no longer breathe, or as the prophet Baruch states "spirit has been taken from their bodies" (Bar 2:17). Likewise, Qoheleth (Teacher) notes, ". . . [T]he dust returns to the earth as it was, and the breath returns to God who gave it" (Eccl 12:7). Idols, often made from the same material as people—dust—are not alive because no living spirit was breathed into them (Wis 15:11). The author of the HB (OT) book of Numbers presents Moses and Aaron addressing God as "the God of the spirits of all flesh" (Num 16:22), and later in the book Moses alone addresses "the LORD, the God of the spirits of all flesh" (Num 27:16).

That the breath of life is spirit, and spirit is a sharing in divinity becomes very clear in the HB (OT) book of Job. Job declares, ". . . [A]s long as my breath is in me / and the spirit of God is in my nostrils, / my lips will not speak falsehood . . ." (Job 27:3). In the same book, Elihu, one of Job's friends, aptly summarizes the understanding that breath is divine spirit, stating, "The spirit of God has made me, / and the breath of the Almighty gives me life" (Job 33:4). Later, he adds, "If [God] should take back his spirit to himself, / and gather to himself his breath, / all flesh would perish together, / and all mortals return to dust" (Job 34:14–15). The prophet Isaiah also states this presupposition, writing, "Thus says God, the LORD, / who gives breath to the people upon [the earth] / and spirit to those who walk in it" (Isa 42:5). As would be expected, this understanding that breath is life and spirit and sharing in divinity can be found in the CB (NT). The author of Mark's Gospel indicates Jesus' death by stating simply, that he "breathed his last" (Mark 15:37), that is, he gave up his spirit; he died. The author of Matthew's Gospel copied what he found in Mark (Matt 27:50), because it accurately connected breath, spirit, and life. However, the author of Luke's Gospel is more explicit; Jesus says, "Father, into your hands I commend my spirit" (Luke 23:46), before he breathes his last! After his death, the risen Jesus appears to his disciples in John's Gospel; "he breathed on them and said to them, 'Receive the Holy Spirit'" (John 20:22). And with those words, the author has indicated that breath and spirit are one and the same; to breathe is to inhale divine spirit.

Meditation/Journal: In what specific ways have you experienced your breath being Spirit? What divine life did you inhale? What wind blew through you to bring life?

Psalm Response: "What a wildly wonderful world, GOD! / You made it all, with Wisdom at your side, / made earth overflow with your wonderful creation. / If you turned your back [on your creatures], / they'd die in a minute— / Turn back your Spirit and they die, / revert to original mud; / Send out your Spirit and they spring to life— / the whole countryside in bloom and blossom." (Ps 104:24, 29–30)

Baptized

Scripture: "[John the Baptist] proclaimed, 'The one who is more powerful than I is coming after me . . . . I have baptized you with water, but he will baptize you with the Holy Spirit.'" (Mark 1:7–8)

Reflection: The Greek word which gives rise to the English words *baptism* and *baptize* means to dip, to immerse; it implies sprinkling, dunking, or drowning in water. The water baptism which John the Baptist was administering in the Jordan River was one in which John dipped or immersed those who presented themselves to him. As he is portrayed in Mark's Gospel in the CB (NT), he declares that a more-powerful one is coming after him who will baptize—dip, immerse, dunk—with the Holy Spirit, that aspect of God that connects to and directs the spirit of every creature. This is why Jesus was baptized by John in the Jordan River at the beginning of his ministry; he—dipped, immersed, and dunked in the Spirit—went about sharing Spirit with all other spirits he met. In Matthew's Gospel in the CB (NT), the author quotes the Markan John the Baptist, but adds that the more-powerful one will baptize with the Holy Spirit and fire (Matt 3:11). The author of Luke's Gospel contains the same words (Luke 3:16), indicating that both he and the author of Matthew's Gospel had access to the same source, called Q (*quelle*, meaning *source*). The word fire, an element in biblical theophanies, is a sign of the presence of God. Thus, John the Baptist announces that the more-powerful one coming after him will dip, immerse, or dunk people into the divine presence! In other words, they will be in God.

In the Acts of the Apostles, the second volume of Luke's Gospel, Jesus is recorded as telling his apostles that John baptized with water, but they would be baptized with the Holy Spirit (Acts 1:5). Peter recounts those words to Cornelius (Acts 11:16). It is also why the Matthean Jesus tells the eleven apostles to baptize in the name of the Holy Spirit (Matt 28:19). In his First Letter to the Corinthians, Paul expands the dipping and immersing metaphor; he declares that all believers have been baptized into one Spirit and form one body; thus, all drink of one Spirit (1 Cor 12:13). In other words, all who have been baptized in the Spirit have been so immersed in God that they drink God's Spirit. In his letter to the Galatians, Paul compares the experience of the Spirit to being clothed with Christ (Gal 3:27); they have put on, they are covered with, a garment of Christ's Spirit. Like he told the Corinthians, there is no longer Jew or Greek, slave or free, for all are one in the one Spirit (1 Cor 12:13; Gal 3:28). Modern metaphors for being immersed in the Holy Spirit could include jumping into a large swimming pool and being surrounded by water; walking through a dense fog that covers everyone and everything; and realizing that all exist on the third planet from the sun in air, an odorless, colorless gas necessary for life.

Meditation/Journal: What is your favorite metaphor for living in the divine Spirit? As you reflect upon it, what implications do you draw from it? Explain.

Psalm Response: "Is there anyplace I can go to avoid your Spirit [, GOD]? / to be out of your sight? / If I climb to the sky, you're there! / If I go underground, you're there! / If I flew on morning's wings / to the far western horizon, / You'd find me in a minute— / you're already there waiting! (Ps 139:7–10)

ℭ

Children of God

Scripture: ". . . [A]ll who are led by the Spirit of God are children of God. When we cry, 'Abba! Father!' it is that very Spirit bearing witness with our spirit that we are children of God." (Rom 8:14, 15b–16)

Reflection: Through the Spirit, God has adopted people; these are they whom Paul describes in his Letter to the Romans as being led by the Spirit of God, a distinctively Pauline phrase indicating that believers are being carried away by a spiritual force. They, according to Paul, are children of God; the force of the Spirit implies divine intervention. When the Spirit connects to the human spirit, people call upon God as Father; the Aramaic word is Abba. The Spirit bears witness that we are children of God by prompting our spirit to shout enthusiastically to God "Father." In other words, Spirit seeks spirit, just like spirit seeks Spirit. When they connect, children address God as Abba. Spirit seeking spirit or vice-versa is like rain drops falling from the sky and seeking streams, rivers, lakes, and oceans. Just like the HB (OT) idea that the LORD had adopted the nation of Israel as his chosen people, Paul writes that both adults and children call God Father, as the Spirit confirms that they belong to God. God's Spirit connected to our human spirit bear witness that believers are in fact children of God.

In his letter to the Galatians, Paul writes the same idea. ". . . [B]ecause you are children," he states, "God has sent the Spirit of his Son into our hearts, crying, 'Abba! Father!' So if you are . . . a child, . . . then also an heir, through God" (Gal 4:6–7). A change in status has occurred, according to Paul. Being able to address God as Father, like Jesus did (Mark 14:36), puts us on the same level as Jesus; that means that we are heirs in the same way as Jesus: eternal life. As children of God, the Spirit connects to human spirits, and like Jesus, we call God Father. In other words, with the activity (agency) of the Spirit in human spirits, Jesus' form of address to God (Father) is available to all believers along with all else that Jesus has inherited from God.

Meditation/Journal: In what specific ways has the Spirit led you? What is your favorite form of address to God?

Psalm Response: "Stories we heard from our fathers, / counsel we learned at our mother's knee, / We're not keeping this to ourselves, / we're passing it along to the next generation— / GOD's fame and fortune, / the marvelous things he has done. / He planted a witness in Jacob, / set his Word firmly in Israel, / Then commanded our parents / to teach it to their children / So the next generation would know, / and all generations to come— / Know the truth and tell the stories / so their children can trust in God . . . ." (Ps 78:3–6)

Cloud

Scripture: "While [Peter] was [speaking], a cloud came and overshadowed [Jesus, Peter, John, and James]; and they were terrified as they entered the cloud. Then from the cloud came a voice that said, 'This is my Son, my Chosen, listen to him!'" (Luke 9:34–35)

Reflection: In the HB (OT) book of Exodus, a cloud is a sign of the divine presence. Once the Israelites leave Egypt, the LORD travels in front of the pilgrims as a pillar of cloud by day (Exod 13:21–22). Once Moses leads them to Horeb (Sinai), a thick cloud appears on the mountain (Exod 19:16). When Moses goes up the mountain, a cloud covers it (Exod 24:15–16). Whenever Moses went to the tent of meeting, a pillar of cloud would descend at the entrance to the tent (Exod 33:9–10; 40:34–35). And the cloud lifted from the tent when it was time for the pilgrims to continue their journey to the promised land (Exod 40:36–38). The author of the book of Exodus makes clear that the cloud represents the glory of the LORD (Exod 24:16; 40:34–35), the presence of God, which came to rest in the Jerusalem Temple once King Solomon finished building it and dedicated it (1 Kgs 8:10–11).

In order to echo the cloud that overshadowed Jesus, Peter, John, and James, the author of Luke's Gospel, who is also the author of the Acts of the Apostle, portrays Jesus being lifted up and a cloud hiding him from the sight of his apostles (Acts 1:9) until the day when the Son of Man comes in a cloud with power and great glory (Luke 21:27). In his First Letter to the Corinthians, Paul expresses his opinion that his ancestors were under the cloud and baptized with the Spirit in the cloud (1 Cor 10:1). When the Most High overshadows, like a cloud, the Spirit engulfs one. Moses was engulfed by a thick cloud, as was Jesus. In other words, they were inundated in divine presence.

Meditation/Journal: When have you been engulfed by a thick cloud, like fog, or afternoon clouds in the mountains? How did you feel? Did such overshadowing make you aware of the divine presence (Spirit)?

Psalm Response: "I sing to GOD, the Praise-Lofty, / and find myself safe and saved. / A hostile world! I call to GOD, / I cry to God to help me. / From his palace he hears my call; / my cry brings me right into his presence— / a private audience! / Now he's wrapped himself / in a trenchcoat of black-cloud darkness. / But his cloud-brightness bursts through . . . . (Ps 18:3, 6, 12a)

Comforter

Scripture: ". . . [T]he church throughout Judea, Galilee, and Samaria had peace and was built up. Living in the fear of the Lord and in the comfort of the Holy Spirit, it increased in numbers." (Acts 9:31–32)

Reflection: The two verses above form a summary, which concludes a section of the Acts of the Apostles. The word *church* is a reference to small, local communities of believers, often called assemblies, and not to buildings! Those gatherings of believers live in the fear of the Lord; they are not afraid of God. Rather, they reverence the Lord; they honor and respect him; they live in awe of him; they give him their undivided attention. With a joyful awareness of God's greatness, believers cooperate with him. Living in reverent cooperation, they experience the comfort of the Holy Spirit; in Greek the word is *paraclete*, the one who is called to one's side to assist. Thus, according to the author of the Acts of the Apostles—the same author of Luke's Gospel—the Comforter, the Holy Spirit, stands by the side of believing communities.

As a Comforter, the Holy Spirit relieves the anxieties of those who reverence God in small Christian communities. In other words, the Holy Spirit is like a comforter, a warm quilt used as a bed covering. The lack of a comforter expressed in the HB (OT) book of Lamentations (1:16) and in the prophet Nahum (3:7), according to the Acts of the Apostles, has now been supplied by the Holy Spirit. God himself stands by the side of those who believe that he raised his son, Jesus, to new life. As they reverence him, he covers them, like a comforter, with himself.

Meditation/Journal: In what specific ways have you experienced the Holy Spirit as a Comforter?

Psalm Response: "God, answer in love! Answer with your sure salvation! / Now answer me, GOD, because you love me; / Let me see your great mercy full-face. / I'm broken . . . , / Flat on my face, reduced to a nothing. / I looked in vain for one friendly face. Not one. / I couldn't find one shoulder to cry on. / Let me shout God's name with a praising song, / Let me tell his greatness in a prayer of thanks." (Ps 69:13b, 16, 20, 30)

𝔇

Demons Cast Out

Scripture: Jesus said, ". . . [I]f it is by the Spirit of God that I cast out demons, then the kingdom of God has come to you." (Matt 12:28)

Reflection: In the world of Jesus, a demon was any kind of illness, infection, addiction, epileptic seizure, etc. that afflicted people but was not understood, as we do today. A person possessed by a demon was one who was sick physically, mentally, spiritually, or psychologically. In the earliest gospel of Mark, the author presents his Jesus character as one who casts out demons, that is, he heals people. In Mark's Gospel, the demons are often referred to as unclean spirits who, in contrast with disciples—who do not know who he is—know Jesus' origins. That theme permeates Mark's Gospel (Mark 1:23–27, 30–31, 32, 34; 3:11, 30; 5:2, 8, 12, 13; 6:7; 7:25; 9:25). The Markan Jesus merely orders the demon to leave a person, and, after identifying Jesus, the unclean spirit obeys him, while the disciples are amazed! However, in Matthew's Gospel, as is presented in the above Scripture text, Jesus declares that it is by the Spirit of God that he casts out demons, a sign that the kingdom of God has come. There is a parallel saying in Luke's Gospel—indicating that the saying's origin is Q—in which the Lukan Jesus states that it is by the finger of God that he casts out demons (Luke 11:20). The author of Luke's Gospel has a knowledge of the HB (OT). The image of the finger of God is found in the HB (OT) book of Exodus, where the finger of God inscribes the tablets (Exod 31:18). In his Second Letter to the Corinthians, Paul combines the image of the finger of God and the Spirit of God, telling his readers that they are his letter of recommendation, "written not with ink but with the Spirit of the living God (finger), not on tablets of stone but on tablets of human hearts" (2 Cor 3:3). Nevertheless, the casting out of demons with the Holy Spirit in Matthew's Gospel is a manifestation that the kingdom of God is present in the healing done by Jesus of Nazareth.

Meditation/Journal: What do you consider to be modern demons (unclean spirits) that need to be removed from people? Who casts out (heals) modern demons? In what ways do those healed of modern demons manifest the kingdom of God?

Psalm Response: "I look up at your macro-skies, [GOD,] dark and enormous, / your handmade sky-jewelry, / Moon and stars mounted in their settings. / Then I look at my micro-self and wonder, / Why do you bother with us? / Why take a second look our way? / GOD, brilliant Lord, / your name echoes around the world." (Ps 8:3–4, 9)

Dewfall

Scripture: Hushai said to Absolom, ". . . [W]e shall come upon [David] in whatever place he may be found, and we shall light on him as the dew falls on the ground; and he shall not survive, nor will any of those with him." (2 Sam 17:12)

Reflection: The word *dewfall* is an oxymoron—a figure of speech that juxtaposes concepts with opposite meanings within a word that is a self-contradiction. While ancient people thought that dew fell from the sky, like rain, today we know that dew is formed by the condensation of water on grass and other objects; condensation is the process a material undergoes when it changes from a gas to a liquid. Thus, dew is the result of water changing from a vapor to a liquid when temperatures drop and grass and other objects cool. However, ancient people did not know this! They lived in a three-storied universe; the underworld is where the dead lived; the flat, plate-like surface of the earth is where people lived; and above the heavens is where God lived. Since rain fell from the heavens at God's command, ancient people thought that dew, being a type of moisture, also fell from the heavens. In King David's son Absalom's attempt to overthrow his father and rule in his father's place, Absalom receives counsel from Hushai, who tells him to gather all the tribes of Israel and set out to find David, who has fled Jerusalem, and catch him by surprise, falling on him like dew falls on the ground. The author of the OT (A) book of Wisdom sees the planet from God's perspective, writing that the whole world before God is like a speck that tips the scales, / "and like a drop of morning dew that falls on the ground" (Wis 11:22).

Because dew is moisture, both the prophets Isaiah and Hosea use it as a metaphor for life. In a hymn of praise to God, Isaiah writes that God's "dead shall live, their corpses shall rise" (Isa 26:19a). Addressing the dead, the prophet states, "O dwellers in the dust, awake and sing for joy! / For your dew is a radiant dew, / and the earth will give birth to those long dead" (Isa 26:19). A radiant dew is one that gives light; the dead will no longer be confined to the darkness of the dirt and the underworld. Just as dew renews plant life, God promises new life to his people. Hosea records the LORD stating, "I will be like the dew to Israel; / he shall blossom like the lily, / he shall strike root like the forests of Lebanon" (Hos 14:5). In other words, the nation will be revived or reborn, like dew promotes life and growth. The imagery of dewfall that gives life—even to the dead—is found in *The Roman Missal*'s Eucharistic Prayer II; the priest or bishop prays to God, asking him to send the Spirit upon the gifts of bread and wine, like the dewfall, to make them the body and blood of Christ. In other words, the Holy Spirit enlivens bread and wine, making them the radiant presence of Christ; thus, whoever eats the bread and drinks the wine is given divine (eternal) life (John 6:33) and will live forever (John 6:51, 56).

Meditation/Journal: What truth do you discover in the oxymoron *dewfall*?

Psalm Response: "How wonderful, how beautiful, / when brothers and sisters get along! / It's like the dew on Mount Hermon / flowing down the slopes of Zion. / Yes, that's where GOD commands the blessing, / ordains eternal life." (Ps 133:1, 3)

Dove

Scripture: "At the end of forty days, Noah . . . sent out the dove from him, to see if the waters had subsided from the face of the ground; but the dove found no place to set its foot, and it returned to him to the ark, for the waters were still on the face of the whole earth. So he put out his hand and took it and brought it into the ark with him. He waited another seven days, and again he sent out the dove from the ark; and the dove came back to him in the evening, and there in its beak was a freshly plucked olive leaf; so Noah knew that the waters had subsided from the earth. Then he waited another seven days, and sent out the dove, and it did not return to him anymore." (Gen 8:6–12)

Reflection: In the Yahwist version of the biblical flood story—there is also a priestly version that has been melded into the Yahwist version—according to the narrator, Noah sends a dove from the ark three times—three is the number representing God (but not Trinity). The first time it returns because there is no place for it to rest; the second time it returns with an olive branch or leaf, a sign of renewed fertility; and the third time it doesn't return because it has found dry ground. The dove is a sign that the water of the great flood has receded, and it is now safe for all in the boat to emerge from it. Since Noah and his family represent the new beginning of humankind—all the humans of the past have been drowned—the dove is also a sign of new life. In the CB (NT) Gospel according to Matthew, Jesus tells his disciples to be as innocent as doves (Matt 10:16). Thus, the dove represents the innocence of new life.

While doves are mentioned elsewhere in biblical literature and winged creatures generally represent the realm of the spiritual biblically, the most striking biblical imagery occurs in Mark's Gospel (70 CE) in the CB (NT). The narrator of the oldest gospel states that after Jesus was baptized by John the Baptist in the Jordan River, "as he was coming up out of the water, he saw the heavens torn apart and the Spirit descending like a dove on him" (Mark 1:10). Then, God speaks, naming Jesus his Son and declaring that he is well pleased (Mark 1:11). According to Mark's Gospel, only Jesus sees the heavens torn apart and the Spirit descending like a dove; only Jesus hears the voice of God. By the time the author of Matthew's Gospel is writing (80 CE), the baptism of Jesus by John had become a controversy; if John baptized Jesus, then the conclusion reached is that John is greater than Jesus, no matter what he says about a more powerful one coming after him (Mark 1:7; Matt 3:11; Luke 3:16). The author of Matthew's Gospel rewrites the baptismal scene he found in Mark by adding dialogue between John and Jesus and presenting Jesus telling John to baptize him to fulfill all righteousness (Matt 3:15), a unique Matthean theme. As Jesus comes up out of the water in Matthew's version, the heavens are opened—not torn apart—and the Spirit of God descends like a dove and alights on him (Matt 3:16), then the voice from heaven claims Jesus as his Son in whom he is well pleased (Matt 3:17). God's announcement is heard by everyone in Matthew's Gospel; it is a combination of Psalm 2:7 ("I will tell of the decree of the LORD: He said to me, 'You are my son; today I have begotten you.'") and Isaiah 42:1ab ("Here is my servant, whom I uphold, / my chosen, in whom my soul delights; / I have put my spirit upon him . . . ."). Ten years later (80 CE), when the author of Luke's Gospel is writing, the controversy about John's and Jesus' greatness has reached a crescendo. Thus, before Jesus is baptized, John the Baptist is imprisoned (Luke 3:20). When the author of Luke's Gospel rewrites the narrative about Jesus' baptism he found in Mark, he inserts one of his favorite themes about praying (Luke 3:21). Then, the heaven opens and the Holy Spirit—notice the name—descends upon Jesus in bodily form like a dove (Luke 3:22). In the Lukan understanding of Jesus' baptism, it is the Holy Spirit who baptizes Jesus of Nazareth (Luke 4:18; Acts 10:38), just like the Spirit confirmed the election of Saul and David as kings of Israel (1 Sam 10:1, 9–10; 11:5–15; 16:13). The author of the third gospel intensifies his perspective by stating that the Holy Spirit descends upon Jesus in bodily form—physically—like a dove (Luke 3:22), and then the voice is heard from heaven. Thus, in Luke's Gospel, John the Baptist does not baptize Jesus, and as far as the author is concerned, that solves the problem of who is greater: John or Jesus. Also, for the author of Luke's Gospel Jesus' baptism is an anointing designating him one of God's chosen. Furthermore, just like Noah's dove heralded a second creation, the dove alighting upon Jesus signals a new creation. When John's Gospel is written early in the second century CE, the author presents another tradition that refines the role of John the Baptist. John, who is not credited with baptizing Jesus, testifies that he saw the Spirit descend from heaven like a dove (John 1:32). He also testifies that the one who had sent him to baptize with water (presumably God) had told him that the one upon whom he saw the Spirit descend and remain was the one who baptizes with the Holy Spirit (John 1:33). Thus, in John's Gospel, the dove functions as a sign; it makes Jesus known. There is no voice from heaven. The visible sign of the Spirit, the dove, indicates the love ("beloved" in Mark 1:11; Matt 3:17; Luke 3:22b) of the Father for the Son.

Meditation/Journal: What does a dove signify for you? What is your response to the reflection on the decreasing of the importance of John the Baptist and the increasing of the importance of Jesus by gospel writers over the span of about forty years?

Psalm Response: "Open your ears, God, to my prayer; / don't pretend you don't hear me knocking. / I shake with fear, / I shudder from head to foot. / 'Who will give me wings,' I ask— / 'wings like a dove?' / Get me out of here on dove wings; / I want some peace and quiet." (Ps 55:1, 5–7)

Ⅎ

Emmanuel

Scripture: ". . . [A]n angel of the Lord appeared to [Joseph] in a dream and said, '. . . [D]o not be afraid to take Mary as your wife, for the child conceived in her is from the Holy Spirit.' All this took place to fulfill what had been spoken by the Lord through the prophet: 'Look, the virgin shall conceive and bear a son, / and they shall name him Emmanuel,' which means, 'God is with us.'" (Matt 1:20, 23)

Reflection: In the CB (NT) Gospel according to Matthew, the name *Emmanuel* is spelled with an E. In the author's source—Isaiah—the name *Immanuel* is spelled with an I. In Isaiah, the young woman will give birth to a son and name him Immanuel (Isa 7:14); Immanuel, like other names of children in the Bible, is a sign that God is with his people. In 735 BCE, King Ahaz of Judah was facing an attack by King Pekah of Israel and King Rezin of Damascus to force Judah into an alliance against powerful Assyria. However, Ahaz intended to enter an alliance with Assyria. The prophet Isaiah offered Ahaz a sign that the campaign of Pekah and Rezin would be unsuccessful. The sign was a male child named Immanuel; his birth meant that Ahaz was right to enter an alliance with Assyria; in other words, God was with him. The name reflects the understanding that the LORD was with his people in his Temple in Jerusalem. In Isaiah 8:8, the prophet addresses the child, stating that Judah can take comfort in God's promise of protection. The LORD protects Jerusalem from enemy kings. Ahaz does not need to fear the plot of Pekah, Rezin, and their allies. He needs only to trust in God's promise to be with him and the people he rules.

The author of Matthew's Gospel removes the historical context of Isaiah's words and uses them to introduce Jesus' birth narrative. Twice the narrator of Matthew's Gospel states that Mary was found to be with child from the Holy Spirit (Matt 1:18, 20). Although Joseph is told to name the child Jesus by the angel (Matt 1:21), the narrator states that Isaiah's words were fulfilled by naming him Emmanuel (Matt 1:23). The meaning of Emmanuel, "God is with us" (Matt 1:23), introduces a unique Matthean theme (Matt 17:17; 18:20; 26:29), which reaches a crescendo and forms an inclusion at Matthew 28:20, where Jesus tells his disciples, ". . . I am with you always, to the end of the age"; in other words, God is with us. But the risen Christ is not with us bodily; he is with us as Spirit. He was generated by the Holy Spirit, God's creative intervention. Furthermore, at the end of the gospel, the Matthean Jesus has told his disciples to make disciples and baptize them in the name of the Holy Spirit (Matt 28:19). While the author does not identify Jesus as God, Jesus is the form in which God was present with his people while Jesus walked the earth, and the Holy Spirit is the form in which he continues to be God with us (Emmanuel, Immanuel).

Meditation/Journal: In what ways is God with you? What name(s) do you give to that presence?

Psalm Response: "God is a safe place to hide, / ready to help when we need him. / Jacob-wrestling God fights for us, / GOD-of-Angel-Armies protects us. / Attention, all! See the marvels of GOD! / Jacob-wrestling God fights for us, / GOD-of-Angel-Armies protects us." (Ps 46:1, 7–8, 11)

Eternal Spirit

Scripture: ". . . [I]f the blood of goats and bulls, with the sprinkling of the ashes of a heifer, sanctifies those who have been defiled so that their flesh is purified, how much more will the blood of Christ, who through the eternal Spirit offered himself without blemish to God, purify our conscience from dead works to worship the living God!" (Heb 9:13–14)

Reflection: The mis-named Letter to the Hebrews is better understood as a sermon, homily, or thesis on Jesus as a high priest superior to those of the past. After noting that in the past the high priests offered the blood of goats and bulls and sprinkled the ashes of a heifer to cleanse, purify, and sanctify those who had somehow been defiled in their flesh, he uses the biblical argument "how much more" to demonstrate that the blood of Christ offered by unblemished Jesus himself through the eternal spirit to God—a superior high priest—purifies internally—the conscience—from sin in order to set free people to worship the living God. In other words, what the former high priesthood was unable to do—purify the conscience—Jesus' high priesthood accomplished. With the arrival of Christ as high priest, according to the author of Hebrews, Jesus did not offer to God other sacrificial victims; he offered himself to God through the eternal Spirit, one that lasts for all time without beginning or end. This idea will later, in Christian history, be used to capture the meaning of the doctrine of the Trinity: one eternal God, three divine persons.

According to Hebrews, the means of Jesus' self-offering to God is the eternal Spirit. The author of Hebrews contrasts Jesus once-for-all offering of himself with previous high priests, who had to make atonement for their sins repeatedly. Christ's offering of himself did not take place at the Jerusalem Temple, but in the spiritual or heavenly dwelling place of God. He did not use the blood of animals; he used his own blood. In other words, he joined his spirit to the eternal Spirit and offered what was most truly himself. It was a spiritual offering; he offered to God the very Spirit God had given to him. That Spirit-laden offering accomplished—enabled—what no previous high-priest's offering could accomplish; it purified the interior spirit of people so that they could worship freely (without sin) the living God. In other words, it accomplished atonement.

Meditation/Journal: What does the eternal Spirit enable in you? What aspect of the author of Hebrews presentation catch most of your attention? Explain.

Psalm Response: "GOD, investigate my life; / get all the facts firsthand. / I am an open book to you; / even from a distance, you know what I'm thinking. / Is there anyplace I can go to avoid your Spirit? / to be out of your sight? / If I climb to the sky, you're there! / If I go underground, you're there! / If I flew on morning's wings / to the far western horizon, / You'd fine me in a minute— / you're already there waiting." (Ps 139:1–2, 7–10)

ℱ

ℱear of the Lord

Scripture: "The spirit of those who fear the Lord will live, / for their hope is in him who saves them." (Sir 34:14–15)

Reflection: Most people respond to the word *fear* with anxiety. Such an unpleasant feeling of apprehension or distress is caused by the presence or anticipation of God. However, biblically the fear of the Lord or the fear of God is understood positively. The fear of the Lord implies awe and reverence; it is a major biblical theme, implying a follower of God. In the HB (OT) book of Deuteronomy, the question is asked: ". . . O Israel, what does the LORD your God require of you?" Then, Moses answers: "Only to fear the Lord your God, to walk in all his ways, to love him, to serve the LORD your God with all your heart and with all your soul, and to keep the commandment of the LORD your God and his decrees that I am commanding you today, for your own well-being" (Deut 10:12–13). The prophet Malachi, in reference to the priests, characterizes the fear of the LORD as "a covenant of life and well-being" which "called for reverence" and standing "in awe of [the LORD's] name" (Mal 2:5).

This positive understanding of fear as reverence and awe comes from an experience of the transcendence of God. Such an experience is described by the prophet Isaiah (6:1–4). The prophet's experience of the LORD is awe to such a degree that he laments seeing God because he is a sinful man. However, his reverence enables the LORD to blot out his sin. Isaiah responds to God's question, "Whom shall I send?" by replying, "Here am I; send me!" (Isa 6:8) When the divine Spirit makes an intimate connection to the human spirit, the results are reverence and awe. Spiritual well-being occurs; in other words, spirituality is enhanced or intensified, and a person feels awe and reverence for God. The author of the Acts of the Apostles—the same person who wrote Luke's Gospel—presents a summary statement about the earliest followers of Jesus in Judea, Galilee, and Samaria. He writes that they were living in the fear of the Lord and increasing in numbers (Acts 9:31). As more and more people experienced the positive fear of the LORD, numbers increased of those who placed their hope in him to save them.

Meditation/Journal: What is your initial response to the phrase *fear of the Lord*? When have you recently experienced God and entered a state of awe and reverence? Explain.

Psalm Response: "I waited and waited and waited for GOD. / At last he looked; finally he listened. / He taught me how to sing the latest God-song, / a praise-song to our God. / More and more people are seeing this: / they enter the mystery, / abandoning themselves to GOD. / Blessed are you who give yourselves over to GOD . . . ." (Ps 40:1, 3–4a)

𝔉ire/Flame

Scripture: "Divided tongues, as of fire, appeared among [the apostles], and a tongue rested on each of them. All of them were filled with the Holy Spirit . . . ." (Acts 2:3–4)

Reflection: Throughout biblical literature, fire is a sign of God. In iconography depicting the above Scripture passage, the apostles are seated or standing together in a semi-circle on Pentecost with a flame dancing on top of each one's head. The author of the Acts of Apostles—the same person who wrote Luke's Gospel—knows that fire represents divinity. The HB (OT) book of Exodus states that Moses experienced the LORD as non-consuming fire out of a bush (Exod 3:2; Acts 7:30). In one of the prophet Daniel's visions, he sees an Ancient One (God), whose throne was fiery flames with its wheels of burning fire and a stream of fire issued and flowed from his presence (Dan 7:9c–10a). In the three-storied universe of the ancient world—the underworld where the dead lived; the flat, plate-like surface of the earth, where people lived; and the area above the dome of the sky, where God lived—sacrificial animals were burned—made invisible with fire—and, like smoke, rose from the middle (earth) to the top story (God). This is best illustrated by the story of Manoah and his unnamed wife in the HB (OT) book of Judges. The parents of Samson made an offering, and "the flame went up toward heaven" (Judg 13:20). The Davidic song recorded in the HB (OT) Second Book of Samuel states that smoke went up from the LORD's nostrils, "and devouring fire from his mouth; / glowing coals flamed forth from him" (2 Sam 22:9). ". . . [C]oals of fire flamed forth" (2 Sam 22:13). In other words, God is like a fire-breathing dragon! In similar words, the prophet Isaiah states that the LORD will cause his voice to be heard in "a flame of devouring fire" (Isa 30:30). The prophet Ezekiel records the Lord GOD stating that he would kindle a fire in the forest of the Negev that would devour every green and dry tree; "the blazing flame shall not be quenched" (Ezek 20:47). The Song of Song states that flashes of passion "are flashes of fire, / a raging flame" (Song 8:6). The Son of Man in the CB (NT) book of Revelation is depicted as having eyes like a flame of fire (Rev 1:14; 2:18; 19:12).

With that kind of fiery background, the author of the Acts of the Apostles connects the fire and the Holy Spirit to explain what got the apostles aflame. He is drawing on a description of the prophet Elijah, who is described in the OT (A) book of Sirach as "a prophet like fire" (Sir 48:1), and who, after praying to the LORD, watches as "the fire of the LORD fell and consumed the burnt offering, the wood, the stones, and the dust, and even licked up the water that was in the trench" on Mount Carmel (1 Kgs 18:38). The author of Luke's Gospel presents the angel Gabriel telling Zechariah that his son, John the Baptist, will posses the spirit and power of Elijah (Luke 1:17), and John the Baptist tells people that the one coming after him will baptize them with the Holy Spirit and fire (Luke 3:16; Matt 3:11). Even the Lukan Jesus, who is conceived in his mother's womb by the power of the Holy Spirit (Luke 1:35), makes very clear that he "came to bring fire to the earth" and wishes "it were already kindled" (Luke 12:49). The author of Luke's Gospel understands that both John the Baptist's and Jesus' words are fulfilled with the divided tongues, as of fire, resting on each apostle on Pentecost. God has taken possession of them and set them ablaze with his Holy Spirit. They are engulfed in divine spirit.

Meditation/Journal: What is your favorite image for the Holy Spirit? Where do you find fire ablaze in your home? What do those experiences represent to you?

Psalm Response: "I love you, GOD— / you make me strong. / From his palace he hears my call; / my cry brings me right into his presence— / a private audience! / His nostrils flare, bellowing smoke; / his mouth spits fire. / Tongues of fire dart in and out; / he lowers the sky. But his cloud-brightness bursts through, / spraying hailstones and fireballs. / Then GOD thundered out of heaven; / the High God gave a great shout, / spraying hailstones and fireballs." (Ps 18:1, 6, 8–9, 12–13)

ℱull of/Filled with the Holy Spirit

Scripture: ". . . [T]he spirit of the Lord has filled the world, and that which holds all things together knows what is said . . . ." (Wis 1:7)

Reflection: The biblical image of being full of the Holy Spirit or filled with the Holy Spirit begins with the image of being empty, like a glass, jar, or pitcher. Such a kind of vessel holding liquid, is said to be full or filled when it holds as much as possible or when all the empty space has been filled. A person possesses spiritual capacity; when he or she is full or filled with the Spirit, he or she has become spiritually abundant. The image in the OT (A) book of Wisdom is focused on the Spirit filling the empty world. In the HB (OT) book of Exodus, Moses tells the Israelites that Bezalel—meaning *in the shadow of God*—is filled with divine spirit or the Spirit of God, and he is appointed to make furniture for the tabernacle (Exod 35:31). In the Second Book of Kings, the prophet Elisha requests a double share of the prophet Elijah's spirit, which comes from the Spirit (2 Kgs 2:9). The author of the HB (A) book of Sirach states that Elisha was filled with Elijah's spirit or Spirit (Sir 48:12). In other words, the spirit of the Lord that fills the world fills some people more than others, and they are easily recognized.

The image of being full of or filled with the Spirit is exploited by the author of Luke's Gospel and the Acts of the Apostles. With the theme of being full of or filled with the Spirit, the author of Luke-Acts anticipates Pentecost in the Acts by presenting people filled or full of the Spirit in the gospel. In other words, he anticipates Pentecost in the gospel in order to echo it in the Acts, despite what the Johannine author narrates about there not yet being Spirit, because Jesus was not yet glorified (John 7:39)! Thus, in Luke's Gospel, Zechariah is told by Gabriel that his son, John the Baptist, will be filled with the Holy Spirit (Luke 1:15). Mary, the mother of Jesus, is filled with the Holy Spirit—overshadowed (in the shadow of God, like Bezalel)—so that Jesus is a Spirit child (Luke 1:35). Elizabeth is filled with the Holy Spirit (Luke 1:41); Zechariah is filled with the Holy Spirit (Luke 1:67); Simeon is filled with and guided by the Holy Spirit (Luke 2:25–27); the Spirit child Jesus experiences the Holy Spirit descending upon him (Luke 3:22); therefore, he is full of the Holy Spirit (Luke 4:1), filled with the power of the Spirit (Luke 4:14), and declares that the Spirit of the Lord is upon him (Luke 4:18)—a statement of the obvious! Then, in the second volume—Acts of the Apostles—the author presents the apostles filled with the Holy Spirit (Acts 2:4); Peter filled with the Holy Spirit (Acts 4:8); and Peter and John and their friends filled with the Holy Spirit (Acts 4:31). One requirement of the men chosen to wait on tables is that they must be filled with the Spirit (Acts 6:3) of whom Stephen is singled out as one filled with the Holy Spirit (Acts 6:5; 7:55), as is Ananias visiting Saul (Acts 9:17), Barnabas (Acts 11:24), and Saul (Paul) (Acts 13:9). And just to be sure that the reader gets it, the narrator declares both Barnabas and Paul filled with the Holy Spirit (Acts 13:52). According to the author of Luke-Acts, there are many people who have experienced their abundant, spiritual capacity.

Meditation/Journal: What has been your most recent experience of being full or filled with the Holy Spirit? Explain.

Psalm Response: "God, make a fresh start in me, / shape a Genesis week from the chaos of my life. / Don't throw me out with the trash, / or fail to breathe holiness in me. / Bring me back from gray exile, / put a fresh wind in my sails! / Unbutton my lips dear God; / I'll let loose with your praise." (Ps 51:10–12, 15)

G

Gift

Scripture: Jesus said to his disciples, "If you . . . , who are evil, know how to give good gifts to your children, how much more will the heavenly Father give the Holy Spirit to those who ask him!" (Luke 11:13).

Reflection: After teaching his disciple how to pray, the Lukan Jesus presents a commentary on persistence in prayer from which the above verse is taken. Just as parents know how to give good gifts to their children, God the Father will give the Holy Spirit to those who ask him. The author of Luke's Gospel has altered the Q saying, which states that God will give good things to those who ask him (Matt 7:11) to make the verse a commentary on prayer. Thus, God, who will give gifts of daily prayer, forgiveness, and more, will even more give the gift of the Spirit to those who ask him. The key word in the above verse is *give*, and the implied word is *gift*. Because a gift is something that someone gives to another, the Lukan understanding is that the Father gives the Holy Spirit to those who ask him, just like one gives a gift to another. This becomes clear in the second volume of Luke-Acts. Peter acknowledges that the Holy Spirit is a gift (Acts 2:38; 10:45; 15:8). The Holy Spirit is not the exaggerated free gift of modern advertising; any gift worthy of its name is free. The Holy Spirit is God's gift to those who ask him, according to Luke. In his First Letter to the Thessalonians, Paul agrees, stating that God gives the Holy Spirit (1 Thess 4:8).

While Paul states that "the unspiritual do not receive the gifts of God's Spirit" (1 Cor 2:14), he, nevertheless, writes about "spiritual gifts" (1 Cor 12:1), the "varieties of gifts" that come from "the same Spirit" (1 Cor 12:4). These include wisdom, knowledge, faith, healing, miracles, tongues, interpretation of tongues (1 Cor 12:8–10). "All these are activated by one and the same Spirit, who allots to each one individually just as the Spirit chooses" (1 Cor 12:11). The author of the Letter to the Hebrews echoes Paul's words, when he writes that God gives gifts of the Holy Spirit, distributed according to his will (Heb 2:4). After writing in his Second Letter to the Corinthians that God gives his Spirit as a first installment or down payment with the balance to follow (2 Cor 1:22), in his letter to the Romans, Paul states that all have received the first fruits of the Spirit—the first installment—while they groan inwardly awaiting the payment of the balance in full (Rom 8:23). Thus, the Father gives the gift of the Holy Spirit to those who ask him.

Meditation/Journal: When have you asked the Father for the gift of the Holy Spirit? What gift(s) did the Spirit give you? How did you use it?

Psalm Response: "I'm thanking you, GOD, from a full heart, / I'm writing the book on your wonders. / I'm whistling, laughing, and jumping for joy; / I'm singing your song, High God. / Sing your songs to Zion-dwelling GOD, / tell his stories to everyone you meet." (Ps 9:1–2, 11)

Spirit of Glory

Scripture: "If you are reviled for the name of Christ, you are blessed, because the spirit of glory, which is the Spirit of God, is resting on you." (1 Pet 4:14)

Reflection: The unknown author of the First Letter of Peter tells his Christian readers that the spirit of glory—the Holy Spirit—is manifesting himself when they are persecuted. In other words, the author of the First Letter of Peter is turning negative reviling into positive manifestation; this is the biblical oxymoron of "good suffering" or, more appropriate here, "glorious suffering." Using the word *glory*, the author is drawing a parallel with God's manifested glory in the HB (OT) (Exod 16:7; 24:16; 29:43; 40:34, etc.). After Solomon dedicated the Temple, God's manifested glory filled it (1 Kgs 8:10). Thus, according to the author of the First Letter of Peter, just as God's glory manifested itself in the past, especially in the Temple, so God's Spirit rests on Christians and is manifested through their persecution. This means that God is present through his Spirit to suffering Christians. Persecution and suffering are not to be viewed as strange to Christians' way of life; rather, they should rejoice in them, because the experience of persecution and suffering means that they are blessed by the presence of God's Spirit, and they share in his glory.

The author of the CB (NT) First Letter of Peter is drawing upon words of the prophet Isaiah, who writes, "The spirit of the LORD shall rest [on Jesse's shoot]" (Isa 11:2). Since the branch that was supposed to grow from Jesse's stump—King David's father was named Jesse—never continued to blossom (—the last two Davidic kings—Jehoiachin and Zedekiah—died without heirs in Babylonian captivity—), the author of First Peter considers believers to fulfill Isaiah's words; they now possess and manifest the glory of the Spirit of God, when they are persecuted and suffering. The author echoes the words of the Matthean Jesus: "Blessed are those who are persecuted . . . . Blessed are you when people revile you and persecute you and utter all kinds of evil against you falsely . . . . Rejoice and be glad . . ." (Matt 5:10–12; Luke 6:22–23).

Journal/Meditation: Do you agree or disagree with the author of the First Letter of Peter that persecution and suffering are the experience of the glorious presence of God's Spirit? Explain.

Psalm Response: "You're famous for helping; God, give *us* a break. / Your reputation is on the line. / Pull us out of this mess, forgive us our sins— / do what you're famous for doing! / Go public and show the godless world / that they can't kill your servants and get by with it." (Ps 79:9–10)

Seemed Good to the Holy Spirit

Scripture: ". . . [I]t has seemed good to the Holy Spirit and to us to impose on you no further burden than these essentials . . . ." (Acts 15:28)

Reflection: The above verse is taken from the letter sent from Jerusalem to Antioch with Paul, Barnabas, Judas (Barsabbas), and Silas (Acts 15:22) to let believers know that the men did not need to be circumcised. While the issue seems to be null and void to modern people, it was an important question about the Gentiles for the early believers of those who emerged out of Judaism to become followers of Jesus. The meeting to decide the question takes place in Jerusalem, where the apostles and elders meet to discuss whether Gentile men, who were uncircumcised, needed to be circumcised. In Judaism, circumcision is the physical sign in the male flesh of the covenant God entered with Abram (Gen 17:10–14). Some of the Jews argued that since Christianity emerged out of Judaism, anyone desiring to be a Christian had to be circumcised (become Jewish first). Needless to say, Gentile men hoped that the decision would be negative!

The agreement was reached by the apostles and elders in Jerusalem that the Gentiles did not need to undergo circumcision before being baptized. While the male Gentiles were very happy about that decision, the Jewish-Christians were not, even though the formal language of the letter confirms God's agency in the decision. The God who entered covenant with

Abram and made circumcision the sign of that covenant now says that it seems good to the Holy Spirit not to foster the practice of circumcision among the Gentiles. From a Jewish-Christian perspective, this looks like God is changing his mind! From a Gentile perspective, this is the prospect of a very unwelcomed burden being sidetracked! Those deciding this question are confident that their good decision—to change this most important practice—is guided by the Spirit.

Meditation/Journal: What application of this account is appropriate today? Explain.

Psalm Response: "Your love, GOD, is my song, and I'll sing it! / I'm forever telling everyone how faithful you are! / You once said, 'I joined forces with my chosen leader, / I pledge my word to my servant, David . . . . / I'll preserve him eternally in my love, / I'll faithfully do all I so solemnly promised. / Do you think I'd withdraw my holy promise! / or take back words I'd already spoken? / I've given my word, my whole and holy word; / do you think I would lie to David?' But GOD, you did walk off and leave us . . . . / You tore up the promise you made to your servant, you stomped his crown in the mud." (Ps 89:1, 28, 34–35, 38–39)

Spirit of God

Scripture: "Job again took up his discourse and said: '[A]s long as my breath is in me / and the spirit of God is in my nostrils, / my lips will not speak falsehood, / and my tongue will not utter deceit." (Job 27:1, 3–4)

Reflection: In the above passage from the HB (OT) book of Job, the author equates breath and spirit on Job's lips. He does it again when presenting Elihu's first speech. "The spirit of God has made me, / and the breath of the Almighty gives me life" (Job 33:4). As noted above, the word in Hebrew—*ruah*—can mean both breath and spirit. Likewise, the word in Greek—*pneuma*—can mean both breath and spirit. Since everyone on the third planet from the sun breathes, Paul can tell the Romans that they "are in the Spirit, since the Spirit of God dwells in" them (Rom 8:9). This enables him to state that they are led by the Spirit of God (Rom 8:14) and that Christ has accomplished much through him by the power of the Spirit of God (Rom 15:19).

Because everyone breathes Spirit, the Spirit of God searches everything and everyone, even the depths of God, according to Paul. That means that through the Spirit of God all are connected to God. No one comprehends what is truly God's except the Spirit of God (1 Cor 2:10–11). This understanding leads Paul to write that he has the Spirit of God (1 Cor 7:40); therefore, what he teaches comes from divine authority. He reminds the Corinthians that they were washed, sanctified, and justified in the name of the Lord Jesus Christ and in the Spirit of God (1 Cor 6:11). According to the author of the First Letter of John, the way to know the Spirit of God is to hear others confess that Jesus Christ, who came in the flesh, is from God (1 John 4:2). Just like one is seldom conscious of breathing, but breathing nevertheless, so one is seldom conscious of being in the Spirit of God or aware that the Spirit of God dwells within him or her.

Meditation/Journal: Do you equate your breath with the Spirit of God? Explain. Do you consider yourself to be in the Spirit of God? Explain.

Psalm Response: GOD, "I'm an open book to you; / even from a distance, you know what I'm thinking. / You know everything I'm going to say / before I start the first sentence. / Is there anyplace I can go to avoid your Spirit? / to be out of your sight? / If I climb to the sky, you're there! / If I go underground, you're there! / You'd find me in a minute— / you're already there waiting! (Ps 139:2, 4, 7–8, 10)

Spirit of Grace

Scripture: "How much worse punishment do you think will be deserved by those who have spurned the Son of God, profaned the blood of the covenant by which they were sanctified, and outraged the Spirit of grace? (Heb 10:29)

Reflection: The phrase *Spirit of grace* appears only one time in the Bible, and that is in the mis-named Letter to the Hebrews; Hebrews is best understood as an essay or a long sermon. The above verse is a rhetorical question posed after the author's warning about the consequences of sin under the old covenant—death without mercy (Heb 10:28). He asks the reader to think about Christian apostates employing three vivid metaphors. The first asks the reader to think about those who have spurned or trampled upon the Son of God, an act of utter contempt. The second asks the reader to think about those who have profaned or gravely misjudged the blood of the new covenant; it is this new order sealed in Jesus' blood on the cross, like the old covenant sealed in the blood of animals, that provides access to God and to his forgiveness. The mistake of the apostate is to see the blood as unclean. And the third, which concerns us here, asks the reader to think about those who outrage or insult the source of salvation, the Spirit of grace. The phrase *Spirit of grace* evokes the prophetic words of Joel (2:28) and Zechariah (12:10) about the bestowal of the divine Spirit.

The bestowal of the Spirit flows from Christ's sacrificial act (Heb 4:16; 12:15). Thus, according to the unknown author of Hebrews, anyone who rejects the redemption offered by the new covenant deserves a far greater punishment; that is the conclusion the author hopes his readers will reach by answering his rhetorical question. He concludes his warning by declaring, "It is a fearful thing to fall into the hands of the living God" (Heb 10:31). Furthermore, the author thinks that it is impossible to restore again to repentance those who have once shared in the Holy Spirit (Heb 6:4).

Meditation/Journal: What do you think about Hebrews' perspective? Explain.

Psalm Response: "Listen to this prayer of mine, GOD; / pay attention to what I'm asking. / Answer me—you're famous for your answers! / Do what's right for me. / Hurry with your answer, GOD! / I'm nearly at the end of my rope. / Don't turn away; don't ignore me! / That would be certain death. / Teach me how to live to please you, / because you're my God. / Lead me by your blessed Spirit / into cleared and level pastureland." (Ps 143:1, 7, 10)

Grieved Spirit

Scripture: ". . . [Israel] rebelled / and grieved [the LORD's] holy spirit; / therefore he became their enemy; / he himself fought against them." (Isa 63:10).

Reflection: In English, the verb *to grieve* means *to experience intense sorrow* or *great sadness*. In the context of the above verse from the prophet Isaiah, it is used to describe the LORD's Holy Spirit after Israel's rebellion (idolatry). According to the prophet, the LORD experienced such intense sadness with his chosen people that he began to fight against them. In a similar vein, the author of the HB (OT) book of Genesis narrates that the LORD was sorry that he had made humankind "and it grieved him to his heart"

(Gen 6:5). Also, Isaiah compares the compassion offered by the LORD to Jerusalem to "a wife forsaken and grieved in spirit" (Isa 54:6a). Grieving in spirit is experiencing intense sorrow or sadness within because of something without. The LORD's response to his experience of grieving is to turn away from the people he created, according to biblical imagery. The Bible attributes to God what it attributes to people, who experience grieving.

The author of the second-generation, CB (NT) Letter to the Ephesians tells his readers not to "grieve the Holy Spirit of God," with which they were marked with a seal for the day of redemption (Eph 4:30). He is writing about the need for the Ephesians to put away their former way of life—lies, anger, stealing—especially grieving the Holy Spirit (Eph 4:17–32). According to the author of this letter, his readers were marked with the seal of the Holy Spirit (Eph 1:13); as such, they should not offend, vex, irritate, or insult the divine presence dwelling within them individually and in the community. In other words, the author instructs his readers to refrain from causing the Holy Spirit intense sorrow or sadness by their failure to live the new way of life they had embraced. The author of this letter wants his readers to live the pledge they made after hearing the proclamation of the gospel (Eph 1:13). Anything less than that grieves the Holy Spirit.

Meditation/Journal: Have you ever grieved the Holy Spirit? How? If not, how do you think people grieve the Holy Spirit today?

Psalm Response: "[The Israelites] gave witness that God was their rock, / that High God was their redeemer, / But they didn't mean a word of it; / they lied through their teeth the whole time. / And God? Compassionate! / Forgave the sin! Didn't destroy! / Time and again they pushed him to the limit, / provoked Israel's Holy God. / How quickly they forgot what he'd done, / forgot their day of rescue from the enemy." (Ps 78:35–36, 38, 40–42)

H

Helper

Scripture: "Guard the good treasure entrusted to you, with the help of the Holy Spirit living in us." (2 Tim 1:14)

Reflection: In the Second Letter to Timothy, the unknown author tells Timothy to guard and preserve the deposit of faith God has given to him with the help of the Spirit living within him. The author of this letter is familiar with some genuine Pauline concepts, but addresses this correspondence to any leader in the early church, using the name *Timothy* as the addressee. Before the above verse, the author mentions the gift of God—the Holy Spirit—"a spirit of power and of love and of self-discipline" (2 Tim 1:7) Timothy received. Also called the power of God (2 Tim 1:8), the Holy Spirit makes it easier for Timothy to preserve the faith (treasure) entrusted to him. In other words, the Holy Spirit is his live-in helper.

In Paul's genuine letter to the Galatians, he asks his readers if God supplied them with the Spirit through the works of the law or through their belief in what they heard (Gal 3:5). The obvious answer is that the Spirit was given to them as a helper through their faith. In his letter to the Philippians he writes, ". . . I know that through your prayers and the help of the spirit of Jesus Christ [the proclamation of Christ] will turn out for my deliverance" from imprisonment (Phil 1:19). The petitions or prayers the Philippians offer on Paul's behalf make him aware of human assistance. The help of the supply of Jesus' Spirit gives him divine assistance. Thus, he considers both prayer and the Spirit to make it easier for him to proclaim the gospel, even while he is in prison. In other words, the Holy Spirit (the spirit of Jesus Christ) is provided as a helper to Paul.

Meditation/Journal: In what specific ways has the live-in Holy Spirit made it easier for you to live your faith (good treasure)?

Psalm Response: "I love you, GOD— / you make me strong. / I cry to God to help me. / From his palace he hears my call; / my cry brings me right into his presence— / a private audience! / You protect me with salvation-armor; / you hold me up with a firm hand, / caress me with your gentle ways. / You cleared the ground under me / so my footing was firm." (Ps 18:1, 6, 35–36)

Holy Spirit

Scripture: "From morning until evening [Paul] explained the matter to [the local leaders of the Jews in Rome], testifying to the kingdom of God and trying to convince them about Jesus . . . . Some were convinced by what he had said, while others refused to believe. So they disagreed with each other;

and as they were leaving, Paul made one further statement: 'The Holy Spirit was right in saying to your ancestors through the prophet Isaiah, "Go to this people and say, / You will indeed listen, but never understand, / and you will indeed look, but never perceive, / For this people's heart has grown dull, / and their ears are hard of hearing, / and they have shut their eyes; / so that they might not look with their eyes, / and listen with their ears, / and understand with their heart and turn— / and I would heal them." Let it be known to you then that this salvation of God has been sent to the Gentiles; they will listen.'" (Acts 28:23b–28)

Reflection: The author of the Acts of the Apostles in the CB (NT) is also the author of Luke's Gospel. In Luke's Gospel, Jesus is declared to be "a light for revelation to the Gentiles / and for glory to [God's] people Israel" (Luke 2:32). In the Acts of the Apostles, Paul (Saul) brings Jesus to the Jews (Israel) living in Rome. As noted in the above Scripture verses, they are divided by what he says. After quoting and applying to them words written by the prophet Isaiah (6:9–10)—noting that the Holy Spirit was right in what Isaiah wrote to Jewish ancestors—the Lukan Paul reiterates the statement about Jesus being a light for revelation to the Gentiles, who will listen. While there are many biblical references in the HB (OT), OT (A), and CB (NT), to the Holy Spirit, in the above passage Paul attributes inspiration to him. The Holy Spirit connected to Isaiah, just like he connected to Paul to enable him to proclaim that the gospel has been sent to the Gentiles.

The *Holy* of Holy Spirit means separate, wholly other, while indicating divinity. This mysterious or numinous quality of God, holiness, is manifested by glory. Thus, the Holy Spirit is that Spirit which is wholly other than human spirit. Individual holiness is derived from the person's spirit's contact with the Holy Spirit, divinity, breath, wind. This unseen, life-giving force permeates the universe and stimulates (inspires) creativity; it is divine influence that guides individual believers and communities of Jesus' followers. At the beginning of the twentieth century, English translations of the Bible began to use Holy Spirit instead of what had been the standard: Holy Ghost. The change from Ghost to Spirit was due to the use of the word *ghost* to designate the spirit of a dead person. Add to that some of the words often associated with ghost—apparition, phantom, specter, spook, shadow, wraith, etc.—and it is not hard to see why the change from Ghost to Spirit was made in biblical translations.

Meditation/Journal: What words do you associate with Spirit in English? What words do you associate with Ghost in English?

Psalm Response: ". . . I [, Ezra,]. . . said, 'Let me speak in your presence, Lord. If . . . I have found favor with you, send the holy spirit into me, and I will write everything that has happened in the world from the beginning, the things that were written in your law, so that people may be able to find the path, and that those who want to live in the last days may do so.' He answered me and said, '. . . [P]repare for yourself many writing tablets . . . , and I will light in your heart the lamp of understanding, which shall not be put out until what you are about to write is finished.'" (NRSV, 2 Esd 14:19, 22–25)

3

Immortal Spirit

Scripture: ". . . [Y]ou [, O Lord,] love all things that exist, / and detest none of the things that you have made, / for you would not have made anything if you had hated it. / How would anything have endured if you had not willed it? / Or how would anything not called forth by you have been preserved? / You spare all things, for they are yours, O Lord, you who love the living. / For your immortal spirit is in all things." (Wis 11:24—12:1)

Reflection: The verses above come from a section dealing with God's actions toward the Israelites liberated from Egypt and the Egyptians in the OT (A) book of Wisdom. The author explains why he thinks God did not just destroy the Egyptians. The reason the author offers for the Lord not eliminating Egyptians from the world is, first, that he created them; they exist because of him; he would not have made anything if he had hated it. Second, he willed them to exist; he preserved them. Third, he spares all things, because they belong to him. He loves all that lives. And, fourth, his immortal spirit is in all things. The Lord, who is an eternal, immortal spirit has life in himself, being of himself, and shares his life and being with everything and everyone he has created.

This living, incorruptible, invisible, intangible, indivisible God has left his immortal spirit in all things. In other words, there are traces of God everywhere; that is why the author of the HB (OT) book of Genesis declares that people are made in the image of God (Gen 1:26; 2:7). When commenting on the torture and death of seven brothers in the OT (A) Fourth Book of Maccabees, the author notes that all of them "were moved by an immortal spirit of devotion" to die rather than renege on their Judaism (4 Macc 14:6). If God's immortal spirit is in everything and everyone, then there is no thing, no person, no animal, no tree, etc. that does not reveal God in some way. Thus, because God's immortal spirit is in all things and people, he did not destroy the Egyptians; to do so would have implied that he was destroying an aspect of himself.

Meditation/Journal: Where, in whom, or in what do you see God's immortal spirit?

Psalm Response: "Listen to this prayer of mine, GOD; / pay attention to what I'm asking. / Point out the road I must travel; / I'm all ears, all eyes before you. / Teach me how to live to please you, / because you're my God. / Lead me by your blessed Spirit / into cleared and level pastureland." (Ps 143:1, 8, 10)

J

Joy in the Spirit

Scripture: ". . . [T]he kingdom of God is not food and drink but righteousness and peace and joy in the Holy Spirit." (Rom 14:17)

Reflection: The phrase *joy in the Holy Spirit* is found only in the CB (NT) letter of Paul to the Romans. There is a similar phrase in his First Letter to the Thessalonians, where he praises his audience for "receiving the word with joy inspired by the Holy Spirit" (1 Thess 1:6). The word *joy* and the over-sixty other words created from it—joyous, enjoy, rejoice, etc.—attempt to capture the feeling of great happiness, gladdening, taking pleasure in something full and satisfying, or benefiting from the use of something. In his letter to the Galatians, Paul lists joy as the second fruit of the Spirit (Gal 5:22). In its Romans' context, Paul reminds his readers that the freedom to eat or drink more or less freely is not the essence of God's kingdom. According to Paul, God's kingdom consists of doing the right thing because it is the right thing to do, the laying aside of any concept of superiority by individuals and coming together as equals, and basking in the great happiness that comes from the Holy Spirit. In its First Thessalonians' context, Paul gives thanks that the Thessalonians, in spite of their suffering (persecution), received the word Paul spoke to them with joy coming from the Holy Spirit.

Keeping in mind that the author of Luke's Gospel is the same author of the Acts of the Apostles, Jesus is presented uniquely as rejoicing in the Holy Spirit (Luke 10:21) after sending out seventy disciples and then receiving them (Luke 10:1–20). After they give their report to Jesus, the author states that Jesus was carried away by happiness, which turns into a prayer of thanksgiving to the Father (Luke 10:21). Therefore, it should not come as a surprise that the theme of joy in the Holy Spirit appears in the Acts of the Apostles. After Lukan Paul, a missionary, like the seventy in Luke's Gospel, preaches the word successfully to the Gentiles, who accept it, a group of Jews begin a persecution of Paul and his assistant, Barnabas; the two leave the area, "filled with joy and with the Holy Spirit" (Acts 13:52). While the Jews are filled with jealousy (Acts 13:45), the disciples are filled with joy—great happiness—and the Holy Spirit.

Meditation/Journal: What joy in the Holy Spirit have you most recently experienced? Explain. In what specific ways was your joy an experience of God's kingdom?

Prayer: "I thank you, Father, Master of heaven and earth, that you hid these things from the know-it-alls and showed them to these innocent newcomers. Yes, Father, it pleased you to do it this way. I've been given it all by my Father! Only the Father knows who the Son is and only the Son knows who the Father is. The Son can introduce the Father to anyone he wants to." (Luke 10:21–22)

℟

Spirit of Knowledge

Scripture: "A shoot shall come out from the stump of Jesse, / and a branch shall grow out of his roots. / The spirit of the LORD shall rest on him, / the spirit of wisdom and understanding, / the spirit of counsel and might, / the spirit of knowledge and the fear of the LORD. / His delight shall be in the fear of the LORD." (Isa 11:1–3)

Reflection: Biblical scholars usually take one of two positions concerning the naming of the shoot or branch sprouting from Jesse's stump. First, the prophet may be referring to the situation after the Babylonian King Nebuchadnezzar had removed the last Davidic ruler—Zedekiah (2 Kgs 25:1–7)—after his predecessor and nephew—Jehoiachin (2 Kgs 24:10–12)—had been taken by Nebuchadnezzar and held prisoner in Babylon. Isaiah words express the hope that a new king from the father of King David's line—Jesse—would return to Jerusalem to rule. However, this hope was never fulfilled. Both Jehoiachin and Zedekiah died without heirs in Babylonian captivity. Second, some scholars understand Isaiah's words to be a critique of the then-current Davidic, disappointing, and faithless King Ahaz (Isa 7:1–17); the words are a promise that a new David would return to the original ideals of Davidic kingship animated by the LORD's Spirit. The focus here is on the spirit of knowledge that would rest on the Davidic heir. It is important to note that the Spirit of the LORD would rest upon him; he would be guided by God himself. The Spirit would be the new king's source of knowledge of the LORD (Isa 11:9). Knowledge of the LORD implies fear of the LORD, but not being afraid of God. Fear of the Lord is the mark of the pious person, whose behavior is rooted in awe and respect for the divine.

A different understanding of knowledge is presented in the CB (NT) gospel according to John. It begins with the narrator's words in John 3:16 about God's love for the world resulting in his gift of his only Son, "so that everyone who believes in him may not perish but may have eternal life." In 5:24, the Johannine Jesus tells his listeners that those who hear his word and believe in the God who sent him have eternal life. In a prayer he further defines eternal life as knowing the only true God and Jesus, whom God has sent (John 17:3). Jesus' followers must believe that Jesus came from God, the Father, who sent him (John 17:8). Jesus knows the Father, and his disciples know that the Father sent him (John 17:25). That eternal life is believing in God and Jesus, whom God has sent, reaches a crescendo with the first ending of John's Gospel. The narrator states that the words he has recorded "are written so that you [—the reader—] may come to believe that Jesus is the Messiah, the Son of God, and that through believing you may have life in his name (John 20:31). Thus, the Spirit of knowledge is the source of the ability to know the LORD, according to Isaiah; it is also the source of eternal life, according to the author of John's Gospel.

Meditation/Journal: When have you most recently been animated by the Spirit resting on you and guiding you? Explain. How was that experience one of knowing the LORD or experiencing eternal life?

Prayer Response: "Father, / You put [the Son] in charge of everything human / So he might give real and eternal life to all in his charge. / And this is the real and eternal life: / That they know you, / The one and only true God. / And Jesus Christ, whom you sent. / For the message you gave me, I gave them; / And they took it, and were convinced / That I came from you. / They believed that you sent me. / Righteous Father, the world has never known you, / But I have known you, and these disciples know / That you sent me on this mission." (John 17:1a, 2–4, 8, 25)

𝕷

𝕷aying on of Hands

Scripture: ". . . Paul . . . came to Ephesus, where he found some disciples. He said to them, 'Did you receive the Holy Spirit when you became believers?' They replied, 'No, we have not even heard that there is a Holy Spirit.' Then he said, 'Into what then were you baptized?' They answered, 'Into John's baptism.' Paul said, 'John baptized with the baptism of repentance, telling the people to believe in the one who was to come after him, that is, in Jesus.' On hearing this, they were baptized in the name of the Lord Jesus. When Paul had laid his hands on them, the Holy Spirit came upon them . . . ." (Acts 19:1–6)

Reflection: One sign of the Holy Spirit is the laying on of hands. One person who has received the Holy Spirit stretches out a hand or both hands over and on the head of another person to signify the giving of the Holy Spirit, as Paul is described doing in the Scripture text above from the Acts of the Apostles. As he does so, about twelve Ephesians (Acts 19:7) receive the Holy Spirit. According to the author of the Acts of the Apostles, in Ephesus there were disciples of John the Baptist; they had been baptized into his baptism of repentance. Paul gives the typical CB (NT) interpretation of John the Baptist, namely, that people receiving his baptism should believe in the one who was coming after him: Jesus. This gives Paul the open door to tell the group of Ephesians that they need to be baptized in the name of the Lord Jesus, even though neither the CB (NT) in general nor the Acts specifically gives any dominical warrant for baptism in the name of Jesus! Nevertheless, the text expresses a firm bond between some kind of proper water baptism and the reception of the Holy Spirit through the imposition of hands. This text also illustrates how some followers of Jesus—in this case Paul—tried to win over adherents of John the Baptist. There is no doubt that in this text there is an allusion to Jesus' ministry (John the Baptist, Spirit, twelve followers) in the author's narrative about Paul's ministry in Ephesus.

The HB (OT) illustrates that Spirit can be shared. The narrator of the book of Numbers states that the LORD took some of the spirit that was on Moses and put it on seventy elders (Num 11:25). Later in the same book the LORD, "the God of the spirits of all flesh" (Num 27:16), tells Moses to lay his hands upon Joshua, a man in whom is the Spirit (Num 27:18). Moses laid his hands on Joshua and commissioned him as directed by the LORD (Num 27:23). The author of the HB (OT) book of Deuteronomy explains that Joshua was full of the Spirit because Moses had laid his hands on him (Deut 34:9). In other words, the Spirit can be transferred from one person to another through the laying on of hands.

This is best illustrated in the CB (NT) in the Acts of the Apostles, as already noted above. Peter and John travel to Samaria, where there are people who have been baptized in the name of the Lord Jesus, but they have not received the Holy Spirit. When Peter and John lay hands on them, they receive the Holy Spirit (Acts 8:14–17). Later, Ananias, a disciple, was instructed by the Lord to go to Saul (Paul) and lay his hands on him to that he could be filled with the Holy Spirit (Acts 9:10–17). In Antioch, there was a group of Jesus' followers who laid hands on Barnabas and Saul (Paul) and sent them on mission (Acts 13:1–4). While in the Acts there are other instances of leaders and apostles laying their hands on others to share the Spirit with them, the sign becomes widespread in the first century CE, as noted in the First Letter to Timothy (4:14) and the Second Letter to Timothy (1:6).

Meditation/Journal: What sign do you use to indicate that you are sharing Spirit with another person? Who has shared his or her Spirit with you? What sign accompanied the sharing?

Psalm Response: "Come, bless GOD, / all you servants of GOD! / You priests of GOD, posted in the nightwatch / in GOD's shrine, / Lift your praising hands to the Holy Place, / and bless GOD. / In turn, may GOD of Zion bless you— / GOD who made heaven and earth! (Ps 134:1–3)

Led by the Spirit

Scripture: "Jesus, full of the Holy Spirit, returned from the Jordan and was led by the Spirit in the wilderness." (Luke 4:1)

Reflection: Both the author of Luke's Gospel in the CB (NT), as noted in the above Scripture verse, and the author of Matthew's Gospel state that "Jesus was led . . . by the Spirit into the wilderness" (Matt 4:1). Both changed the words—"the Spirit immediately drove him out into the wilderness" (Mark 1:12)—they found in Mark's Gospel, because they used a source common to both of them known as Q. The urgency found in Mark's Gospel— "immediately drove"—is tempered by the word *led,* which means to guide. In other words, the Spirit, received by Jesus at his baptism, connected to his spirit and led (drove) him into the wilderness, where he was tempted, like the Israelites were tempted in the desert after they escaped Egypt. The double use of the Spirit in Luke's Gospel—"full of the Holy Spirit" and "led by the Spirit"—indicates that the Spirit is the initiator of the event and expresses the solidarity of the Messiah and the Spirit.

The kind of Spirit-leadership envisioned by the author of Luke's Gospel and the author of Matthew's Gospel is also expressed by Paul in his letter to the Romans. He writes, ". . . [A]ll who are led by the Spirit of God are children of God" (Rom 8:14), because they have received a spirit of adoption. In his letter to the Galatians, he writes, ". . . [I]f you are led by the Spirit, you are not subject to the law" (Gal 5:18). This Pauline phrase indicates that one is being constrained by a compelling, enthusiastic, divine force. Children of God, according to Paul, do not conduct their lives as the result of personal effort; proper ethical conduct comes not from following Torah, but from following the lead of the Spirit. Like the Lukan Jesus, children of God submit to the Spirit, who leads them.

Meditation/Journal: When have you been led by the Spirit most recently? Explain. To whom or where did the Spirit lead you?

Psalm Response: "I run to you, GOD; I run for dear life. / Don't let me down! / Take me seriously this time! / You're my cave to hide in, / my cliff to climb. / Be my safe leader, / be my true mountain guide. / I've put my life in your hands. / You won't drop me, / you'll never let me down." (Ps 31:1, 3, 5)

Letter Written with Spirit

Scripture: "You yourselves [, Corinthians,] are our letter, written on our hearts, to be known and read by all; and you show that you are a letter of Christ, prepared by us, written not with ink but with the Spirit of the living God, not on tablets of stone but on tablets of human hearts." (2 Cor 3:2–3)

Reflection: The image used by Paul in his Second Letter to the Corinthians is that of a letter, more specifically, a letter of recommendation. Not only was Corinth an international city of prestige and importance, but he considered the congregation there to be a letter written on his heart and Timothy's heart (2 Cor 1:1) to be known and read by all. The fact that Paul wrote two letters—probably more that have been melded together—to the Corinthians emphasizes that point. Also, Paul has in mind the words of Jeremiah the prophet, who records the LORD stating that in future days he would put his law within the house of Israel and write it on their hearts (Jer 31:33). Ancient people understood the heart to be the very core of a person in which God's Spirit is active. By their behavior, the Corinthains demonstrate that they are a letter of Christ. In other words, Paul is the scribe or secretary, but the real author of the letter is Christ, for whom Paul is a minister.

By contrasting ink, usually used to write letters, and Spirit of the living God, Paul not only continues the letter imagery, but he indicates that the living, human, Corinthian letter (church) is God's life-giving work or new creation. In other words, God works by means of the Spirit. Christ, whose Spirit lives in human hearts, is the content of the letter of recommendation. This makes Paul's best letter of recommendation the Corinthian church or congregation. The letter is not written on stone tablets, like the law was (Exod 24:12; 31:18; 34:1; Deut 9:10–11), but on tablets of human hearts, the Corinthians themselves.

Meditation/Journal: Who has been a letter of Christ written with the Spirit of the living God for you? For whom have you been a letter of Christ written with the Spirit of the living God? Explain.

Canticle Response: "Blessed be the Lord, the God of Israel; / he came and set his people free. / He set the power of salvation in the center of our lives,

/ Just as he promised long ago / through the preaching of his holy prophets: Mercy to our fathers, / as he remembers to do what he said he'd do, / So we can worship him without a care in the world, made holy before him as long as we live." (Luke 1:68–69a, 70, 72, 75)

Spirit Gives Life

Scripture: Jesus said to his disciples, "It is the spirit that gives life . . . . The words that I have spoken to you are spirit and life." (John 6:63)

Reflection: The above verse is part of Jesus' discussion with disciples (John 6:60–71) after he finishes what is called the bread of life discourse (John 6:25–65). The Johannine Jesus, who has come from God and will return to God, knows God; Spirit touching spirit brings people into relationship with the Father. The life-giving power of the Spirit is made available to Jesus' disciples through the revelation of God in the words of Jesus. The author of John's Gospel finds the words of the Lord GOD recorded in the prophet Ezekiel—"I will . . . put a new spirit within them" (Ezek 11:19; 36:26)—fulfilled in Jesus. Paul, too, in his letter to the Romans takes it one step further, writing that those who believe in Jesus are discharged from the law and live in the new life of the Spirit (Rom 7:6). Those in Christ Jesus have been set free from the law of sin and death and live according to the law of the Spirit (Rom 8:2). They set their mind on the life-giving Spirit (Rom 8:6). Like the Johannine author, "the Spirit is life" for Paul (Rom 8:10). In his Second Letter to the Corinthians, he states that the letter of the previous covenant (law, Torah) kills, but the Spirit gives life (2 Cor 3:6). The new covenant has nothing to do with written Torah; the new covenant is one with the active Spirit of the living God.

In his First Letter to the Corinthians, Paul compares the first Adam to the last Adam (Jesus). Paraphrasing the HB (OT) book of Genesis, which states, "the LORD God . . . breathed into [the man's] nostrils the breath of life; and the man became a living being" (Gen 2:7), Paul writes, "Thus it is written, 'The first man, Adam, became a living being'; the last Adam became a life-giving spirit" (1 Cor 15:45). The last Adam, Christ, became a life-giving Spirit through his resurrection from the dead, a spiritual or heavenly experience (1 Cor 15:46–49). The first Adam, an antitype, a natural man, received life; the last Adam, a Spirit-type, an inspired man, gave life once the Spirit gave new life (resurrection) to him.

Meditation/Journal: For you, how does the Spirit give life? What are your reflections on Paul's comparison of the first Adam and the last Adam?

Psalm Response: "Tell me, what's going on, GOD? / How long do I have to live? / Give me the bad news! / You've kept me on pretty short rations; / my life is string too short to be saved. / Oh! We're all puffs of air. / Oh! We're all shadows in a campfire. / Oh! We're just spit in the wind. / We make our pile, and then we leave it. / Ah, GOD, listen to my prayer, my / cry—open your ears. I am a stranger here. I don't know my way— / a migrant like my whole family. / Give me a break, cut me some slack / before it's too late and I'm out of here." (Ps 39:4–6, 12–13)

ℒive by the Spirit

Scripture: "If we live by the Spirit, let us also be guided by the Spirit." (Gal 5:25)

Reflection: In his letter to the Galatians, Paul writes about life in the Spirit. After presenting a list of behaviors that are opposed to life in the Spirit (Gal 5:19–21), he presents what he calls the fruit of the Spirit (Gal 5:22–23). Living in the Spirit for Paul is acknowledging the different gifts and mutual need in the community. He told the community in Rome, ". . . [T]hose who live according to the Spirit set their minds on the things of the Spirit" (Rom 8:5). In his First Letter to the Corinthians, he presents a list of the variety of gifts that come from the Spirit in the community; each gift is for the common good (1 Cor 12:1–31). "Live by the Spirit," he tells the Galatians, "and do not gratify the desires of the flesh" (Gal 5:16), because what gratifies the flesh is opposed to the Spirit (Gal 5:17). Living in the Spirit is like swimming in the ocean; on the earth, people are swimming in the invisible, breath-like, wind-like, air-like Spirit. The more they become aware of the Spirit's presence, the better life they live by the Spirit.

The author of the First Letter of Peter presents Christ, who "was put to death in the flesh, but made alive in the Spirit, in which also he went and made a proclamation to the spirits in prison" (1 Pet 3:18–19). After exhorting his readers to live the rest of their earthly lives no longer by human desires, but by the will of God, even though their fellow citizens in Greco-Roman culture are surprised that they no longer join them (1 Pet 4:4), the author states that God's final judgment will vindicate their new way of life.

Just as Christ in his suffering acted in accordance with God's will, states the author, so must Christians, who have been converted from their former way of life, even if it means ostracization and persecution. According to the author, one day they will have to give an account when they stand before the judge of the living and the dead. Then, he explains what he meant by Christ who made a proclamation to the spirits in prison (1 Pet 3:19). In a three-storied universe, the first story (underground, called Sheol) is where the dead live. ". . . [T]he gospel was proclaimed even to the dead," states the author, "through they had been judged in the flesh as everyone is judged, [so] they might live in the Spirit as God does" (1 Pet 4:6). Those in Sheol are those who died before Jesus, who died before hearing the gospel, or those who died before Christ returned. According to First Peter, after Jesus died, he went to Sheol to evangelize those living there. According to the author, "[t]he end of all things is near" (1 Pet 4:7); in other words, he thinks that judgment day is imminent. Because everyone living in Sheol and on the earth (second level) will be judged, all have been given the opportunity to "live in the Spirit as God does" (1 Pet 4:6). This Petrine understanding gave rise to the phrase about Jesus Christ descending to the realm of the dead in the Apostles' Creed. The author of the letter to the Ephesians states that he "descended into the lower parts of the earth" (Eph 4:9), which is more biblically accurate than the contemporary phrase "he descended into hell."

Meditation/Journal: Specifically, how do you live by the Spirit? How has the Spirit guided you?

Psalm Response: "Is there anyplace I can go to avoid your Spirit [, GOD]? / to be out of your sight? / If I climb to the sky, you're there! / If I go underground, you're there! / If I flew on morning's wings / to the far western horizon, / You'd find me in a minute— / you're already there waiting! (Ps 139:7–10)

Spirit of the Living God

Scripture: ". . . [Y]ou [, Corinthians,] show that you are a letter of Christ, prepared by us, written not with ink but with the Spirit of the living God . . . ." (2 Cor 3:3)

Reflection: As was noted above in "Letter Written with Spirit," in Paul's Second Letter to the Corinthains, the apostle mentions the Spirit of the living

God; the phrase *Spirit of the living God* occurs only here in all of the Bible. In Pauline thought, the phrase refers to the Spirit who comes from and represents the God who is alive. The phrase *Spirit of God* is found throughout the Bible. For example, in the HB (OT) book of Genesis, Pharaoh, after being introduced to and impressed by Joseph, son of Jacob, asks his servants, "Can we find anyone else like this—one in whom is the spirit of God?" (Gen 41:38) Likewise, in the HB (OT) book of Numbers there is Balaam upon whom came the Spirit of God (Num 24:2). Balaam was brought to curse the Israelites, but the living God does as he pleases and stimulates Balaam to bless the Israelites! The judge-prophet-priest Samuel was possessed by the Spirit of God (1 Sam 10:10), as was the first king of Israel he anointed, Saul (1 Sam 11:6; 19:23), and Saul's messengers (1 Sam 19:20). Like Samuel, the Spirit of God came upon Azariah, son of Oded (2 Chr 15:1) and took possession of Zechariah, son of the priest Jehoida (2 Chr 24:20).

In the CB (NT), Paul features the Spirit of God in his letter to the Romans. He tells his readers that the Spirit of God dwells in them (Rom 8:9), they are led by the Spirit of God (Rom 8:14), and he has been enabled by the power of the Spirit of God to proclaim the good news (Rom 15:19). He writes to the Corinthians, telling them that no one comprehends what is truly God's except the Spirit of God (1 Cor 2:11), after telling them they were washed, sanctified, and justified in the name of the Lord Jesus Christ and in the Spirit of our God (1 Cor 6:11). Also in his First Letter to the Corinthians, Paul states that they have received the Spirit that is from God, so that they may understand the gifts bestowed on them by God (1 Cor 2:12). Having the mind of Christ, according to Paul, means the Corinthians are guided by God's Spirit to seek what is truly God's (1 Cor 2:11, 16; Phil 2:5).

Meditation/Journal: Narrate the experiences of the Spirit of the living God you have had. What conclusions can you draw from the narrative of your experiences?

Psalm Response: "I want to drink God, / deep draughts of God. / I'm thirsty for God-alive. / I wonder, 'Will I ever make it— / arrive and drink in God's presence?' / These are the things I go over and over, / emptying out the pockets of my life." (Ps 42:1b–2, 4a)

Spirit of the Lord

Scripture: "Now the Lord is the Spirit, and where the Spirit of the Lord is, there is freedom. And all of us, with unveiled faces, seeing the glory of the Lord as though reflected in a mirror, are being transformed into the same image from one degree of glory to another; for this comes from the Lord, the Spirit." (2 Cor 3:17–18)

Reflection: In order to understand the above Scripture text, the reader must know that in Pauline thought Christ (the Lord) is the Spirit. In the section of his Second Letter to the Corinthians, Paul writes about the new covenant, which in Pauline thought is from the Spirit (2 Cor 3:6). Under the new covenant, the Spirit (Christ the Lord) brings freedom from the law, freedom from trying to earn salvation by keeping the 613 precepts of Torah. Christ is experienced through the Spirit in the new covenant. Also, God is the Spirit, or—using the HB (OT) designation—the LORD is the Spirit. It is not inaccurate to understand that the Lord is the Spirit, since the phrase occurs in the Niceno-Constantinopolitan Creed. In that profession of faith, the Holy Spirit is identified as the Lord. Where the Spirit of Christ (who is also the Spirit of God) is, there is the freedom from Torah. It is the Spirit who brings about freedom.

And the Spirit brings glorification. The veil that covered Moses' face (Exod 34:33–35) has been removed, according to Paul (1 Cor 3:16). The veil kept the Israelites from seeing Moses' face, from seeing the glory of God (2 Cor 3:13) that remained on it. Now, however, followers of Christ Jesus, with unveiled faces behold the glory of the Lord Jesus Christ; that glory is like looking into a mirror (reflecting light) and not seeing one's own face, but seeing the face of Christ. At first the image is blurry, but gradually it is transformed from one degree to another; in other words, the blurriness gets clearer with the help of the Spirit. The transformation that happened to Moses's face is available to everyone through the Spirit. To be God's image is to manifest the divine glory, just as Christ did and continues to do through the Spirit. The image is the glorious Christ, who himself went through the process of glory from one degree to another until he reached resurrection, accomplished by the Spirit.

Meditation/Journal: What kinds of transformation has the Spirit accomplished in you? What freedom did you experience?

Psalm Response: "Bravo, GOD, bravo! / Gods and all angels shout, 'Encore!' / In awe before the glory, / in awe before God's visible power. / Stand at attention! / Dress your best to honor him!/ GOD's thunder sets the oak trees dancing / A wild dance, whirling; the pelting rain strips their branches. / We fall to our knees—we call out, 'Glory!'" (Ps 29:1–2, 9)

ℳ

Manifestation of the Spirit

Scripture: "... [T]here are varieties of the gifts, but the same Spirit; and there are varieties of services, but the same Lord; and there are varieties of activities, but it is the same God who activates all of them in everyone. To each is given the manifestation of the Spirit for the common good." (1 Cor 12:4–7)

Reflection: A manifestation is the act of showing or demonstrating something. That is what Paul is presenting in the First Letter to the Corinthians in the CB (NT). The gifts, services, and activities mentioned in the above Scripture passage are ways to describe manifestations of the Spirit. The Pauline list of manifestations of the Spirit include wisdom, knowledge, faith, healing, miracle-working, prophecy, discernment, speaking in tongues, and interpretation of tongues (1 Cor 12:8–10). "All these," according to Paul, "are activated by one and the same Spirit, who allots to each one individually just as the Spirit chooses" (1 Cor 12:11). Earlier in the same letter, Paul had written that his words proclaiming the crucified Jesus Christ were not plausible words of wisdom, "but with a demonstration of the Spirit and of power" (1 Cor 2:4), so that the Corinthians' faith would rest not on his human wisdom, but on the power of God, divine wisdom. The intended purpose of such a variety of gifts in the Corinthian community is to serve the common good. In other words, gifts are given to individual people to use for other members in the community. Paul illustrates this latter point with his image of the body (1 Cor 12:12–30).

Paul's words about the varieties of gifts allotted to each individual in the community to be used to benefit the other members of the community in a harmony of Spirit, is manifested in Johannine literature in a similar way. In John's Gospel, John the Baptist is depicted as presenting two summaries of the gospel (John 3:22–30; 31–36). In the second summary, the Baptizer declares that Jesus, whom God has sent, speaks God's words and "gives the Spirit without measure" (John 3:34). Jesus, as emissary of God—one who has himself received God's Spirit without measure—gives the Spirit to those who accept his witness.

Meditation/Journal: What gift(s) has (have) the Spirit given to you? How do you use it (them) for the common good?

Psalm Response: "God is well-known in Judah; / in Israel, he's a household name. / Do for GOD what you said you'd do— / he is, after all, your God. / Let everyone in town bring offerings / to the One Who Watches our every move." (Ps 76:1, 11)

𝔐ind of the Spirit

Scripture: ". . . [T]he Spirit helps us in our weakness; for we do not know how to pray as we ought, but that very Spirit intercedes with sighs too deep for words. And God, who searches the heart, knows what is the mind of the Spirit, because the Spirit intercedes for the saints according to the will of God." (Rom 8:26–27)

Reflection: The operative metaphor in the above two verses from Paul's letter to the Romans in the CB (NT) is mind. The mind is the center of consciousness that generates thoughts, feelings, ideas, and perceptions and stores knowledge and memories. Because God is one (Father, Son, Holy Spirit), God has one mind, that is why Paul writes about God knowing the mind of the Spirit. Human weakness consists of being unable to say what we need, how to pray as we ought to pray. However, the Spirit, who is connected to our spirit, lends assistance. The heart, the inner center of a human being, the source of will, emotion, and intentionality—in other words, the human spirit—is known to God through the Spirit, who interacts with human sighs (groaning inwardly, Rom 8:23), and who brings them to God with unspoken intercession. Therefore, according to Paul, God knows what the Spirit is thinking. ". . . [N]o one comprehends what is truly God's except the Spirit of God," writes Paul in his First Letter to the Corinthians (2:11). Thus, the Spirit intercedes for all believers. In other words, God communicates with himself through the groans of human weakness—spirit—connected to Spirit, whose mind God knows. People need God to pray from within them. That way, they are praying as they ought, according to the will of God.

In Second Isaiah (40—55), the prophet asks, "Who has directed the spirit of the LORD, or as his counselor has instructed him?" (Isa 40:13) Paul would answer that question by saying that no one, except God himself, directs his Spirit. The understanding that Spirit connects to spirit is found in the HB (OT) book of Proverbs. "The human spirit is the lamp of the LORD," states the proverb, "searching every inmost part" (Prov 20:27). The author of the HB (OT) First Book of Samuel presents God telling Samuel, when he prepared to anoint one of Jesse's sons as king of Israel, ". . . [T]he LORD does not see as mortals see; they look on the outward appearance, but the LORD looks on the heart" (1 Sam 16:7). As already noted above, the heart, the innermost part, the spirit of each person is known to God through the Spirit's connection to spirit. The prayer, and holiness, of all believers is through their ongoing spiritual connection to the Spirit.

Meditation/Journal: How has Spirit helped you (spirit) in your weakness? Explain. How has Spirit helped you to pray? When have you experienced your spirit connected to Spirit? What happened as a result?

Psalm Response: "Keep me safe, O God, / I've run for dear life to you. / I say to GOD, 'Be my Lord!' / Without you, nothing makes sense. / My choice is you, GOD, first and only. / And now I find I'm *your* choice! / The wise counsel GOD gives when I'm awake / is confirmed by my sleeping heart. / Day and night I'll stick with GOD; / I've got a good thing going and I'm not letting go." (Ps 16:1–2, 5, 7–8)

𝕹

𝕹athan

Scripture: ". . . [T]he word of the LORD came to Nathan: Go and tell my servant David: Thus says the LORD: I will made for you a great name, like the name of the great ones of the earth. Moreover the Lord declares to you that the LORD will make you a house. I will raise up your offspring after you, who shall come forth from your body, and I will establish his kingdom." (2 Sam 6:4–5a, 9b, 11b, 12b)

Reflection: The reader will notice immediately that there is no mention of the Spirit in either the title or the Scripture passage above. That, however, does not mean that the Holy Spirit is not present. Most people are familiar with the major prophets—such as Isaiah, Jeremiah, and Ezekiel—but there are many other prophets in the HB (OT) who do not have books named after them. Among those other prophets is Nathan, whose name means *the god gave*; the reference is to the words the LORD gave to the court prophet Nathan. After David becomes king of all Israel, he captures the Jebusite city of Jerusalem and establishes it as his capitol. Then, he builds himself a house (palace) in which to live. As his court prophet, Nathan is the man who advises David about things concerning Israel's God, the LORD. As is noted in the Niceno-Constantinopolitan Creed, the Holy Spirit has spoken through the prophets. And the Holy Spirit speaks through Nathan to David, who wants to build a house (temple) for God. In this first appearance in biblical literature of the prophet Nathan, he tells David to pursue the project (2 Sam 7:1–3; 1 Chr 17:1–2), but during the night the Spirit delivers the word of the LORD to him (2 Sam 7:4–29; 1 Chr 17:3–27). Nathan is commissioned by God to tell David that he does not want a house (temple) built; instead, he will build a house (dynasty) for David. Known among biblical scholars as the everlasting covenant, God promises a Davidic descendant—one of whom will build a temple—forever. The next time Nathan appears with the word of the LORD from the Spirit is after David sleeps with Bathsheba, gets her pregnant, and enacts a plot to get her husband, Uriah, killed in battle (2 Sam 11:1–27). Nathan narrates a parable to David (2 Sam 12:1–6); David recognizes himself in Nathan's words and repents of his crime (2 Sam 12:7–15a). The account of Nathan confronting King David illustrates the freedom the Spirit-filled prophet Nathan had in speaking to the king.

The third and final time Nathan appears in biblical history is at David's death bed. David has not yet named an heir to his throne, but his son Adonijah has laid claim to the monarchy. The author of the First Book of Kings states that Nathan did not side with Adonijah (1 Kings 1:8). Nathan informs Bathsheba, mother of Solomon, that Adonijah has laid claim to the throne, and instructs her to go to David, tell him what is going on, and ask him to name Solomon as his successor (1 Kgs 1:11–21). Just as Bathsheba finishes her mission, Nathan appears before King David, telling him about Adonijah, and listening as he declares Solomon to be his heir (1 Kgs 1:22–37). The king's cabinet usually included a court prophet, like Nathan, who possessed the gift of prophecy given by the Spirit to communicate divine revelation. In other words, Nathan, called by God, does not foretell or pre-dict the future—the usual understanding of a prophet's role—but filled with the Spirit utters the words of the LORD and makes an experience of God immediate.

Meditation/Journal: Who has recently delivered a prophetic word of the LORD to you? Of what did it consist? To whom have you delivered a pro-phetic word of the LORD? Of what did it consist?

Prayer Response: "Who am I, my Master GOD, and what is my family, that you have brought me to this place in life? But that's nothing compared to what's coming, for you've also spoken of my family far into the future, given me a glimpse into tomorrow, my Master GOD! What can I possibly say in the face of all this? You know me, Master GOD, just as I am. You've done all this not because of who I am but because of who you are—out of your very heart!—but you've let me in on it." (2 Sam 7:18–21)

Overshadower

Scripture: "The angel [Gabriel] said to [Mary], 'The Holy Spirit will come upon you, and the power of the Most High will overshadow you; therefore the child to be born will be holy; he will be called Son of God.'" (Luke 1:35)

Reflection: The verb *to overshadow* means to take attention away from somebody or something by appearing more important or interesting. In the above verse from the CB (NT) Gospel according to Luke, Mary is over-shadowed or overcome by the Holy Spirit and the Most High God's power to focus on the child to be born of her: the Son of God. While the image of overshadowing is usually associated with a cloud, as we will see below, it is also associated earlier and biblically with the LORD. In the HB (OT) book of Exodus, the LORD instructs Moses to make a mercy seat—a cover for the ark of the covenant—with cherubim on each end with their wings over-shadowing the mercy seat (Exod 25:17–21; 37:6–9). Wings signify divine protection; thus, God, who sits on the mercy seat, protects or overshadows himself. The author of the misnamed CB (NT) Letter to the Hebrews refers to the ark's cover as "the cherubim of glory overshadowing the mercy seat" (Heb 9:5). The Spirit of the divine or glorious presence is the creative power of God which overshadowed creation (Gen 1:2). Thus, the overshadowing cherubim become an image of the Holy Spirit.

Another overshadowing image of the Holy Spirit is the cloud. The HB (OT) book of Exodus notes that a thick cloud overshadowed Mount Horeb (Sinai), when Moses brought the newly-escaped Hebrews to meet God (Exod 19:16–19). There is also the cloud that covered the tent of meeting, indicating that the glory of the LORD, the presence of God's Spirit, was there (Exod 40:34–35). The author of the OT (A) book of Wisdom notes that "[t]he cloud was seen overshadowing [Israel's] camp" (Wis 19:7). While none of these references explicitly state that the cloud represents the Holy Spirit, the author of Mark's Gospel in the CB (NT) states that at Jesus' transfiguration—the display of his divinity to Peter, James, and John (Mark 9:2)—a cloud overshadows them (Mark 9:6). Matthew, aware that the cloud represents the glory of the LORD, changes the wording he found in Mark's Gospel to a bright cloud overshadowing the three disciples (Matt 17:5). The author of Luke's Gospel keeps what he found in Mark's Gospel about a cloud overshadowing Peter, James, and John (Luke 9:34), because he has already presented it in the annunciation scene above. Thus, God's Holy Spirit action with Mary—divine power replacing masculine begetting—expresses the preeminence of the divine Father's Spirit in the begetting of his Son, Jesus. The child conceived in Mary's womb is called holy, engendered by God, selected by God, and conceived for God. In other words, Jesus is the Son of God and a Spirit child. Paul, who at the time of his writing the Letter to the Romans knows no birth narrative concerning Jesus, states that Jesus "was declared to be Son of God with power according to the spirit of holiness by resurrection from the dead" (Rom 1:4). Paul presents an understanding of the role of the Spirit at Jesus' resurrection that gets moved back to his conception in Matthew (1:18,20) and, especially, in Luke (1:35) and is demonstrated with the overshadowing cloud at his transfiguration by all three synoptic authors.

Meditation/Journal: When have you been overshadowed by the Holy Spirit? To what did you give birth?

Psalm Response: "You who sit down in the High God's presence, / spend the night in Shaddai's shadow, / Say this: 'God, you're my refuge. / I trust in you and I'm safe!' / That's right—he rescues you from hidden traps, / shields you from deadly hazards. / His huge outstretched arms protect you— / under them you're perfectly safe; / his arms fend off all harm. / You'll stand untouched, watch it all from a distance . . . . / Yes, because GOD's your refuge, / the High God your very own home." (Ps 91:1–4, 7, 9)

𝔓

𝔓araclete

Scripture: Jesus said to his disciples, "Do not let your hearts be troubled. Believe in God, believe also in me. . . . I will ask the Father, and he will give you another Advocate, to be with you forever. This is the Spirit of truth . . . ." (John 14:1, 16)

Reflection: In Greek, the original language of the CB (NT), the word is *Paraclete*, as is often found in older Bibles. When the Greek text is translated into Latin, the word is *Advocatus*. And when the Latin word is translated into English, it becomes *Advocate*. *Paraclete*, used in Johannine—John's Gospel; First, Second, and Third Letters of John—literature, is a legal word, meaning to call one to stand beside another, to help in a lawcourt, to help a person represent himself or herself before a judge. *Advocatus*, used to translate the Greek *Paraclete* into Latin, is also a legal term, indicating a person of high social standing who speaks on behalf of a defendant in a court of law before a judge. When older Bibles printed *Paraclete*, the translators had merely transliterated—represented the letters of the word from the Greek alphabet with corresponding letters in the English alphabet. Modern Bible translators translate the Greek word *Paraclete* into *Advocate*, obviously using the Latin word *Advocatus* for help, as seen in the above Scripture text.

In addition to the use of *Paraclete* in the above verse, the word appears three more times in John's Gospel and one time in the First Letter of John. In chapter 14 of John's Gospel, Jesus tells his disciples, ". . . [T]he Advocate, the Holy Spirit, whom the Father will send in my name, will teach you everything." (John 14:26). Later he tells them, "When the Advocate comes, whom I will send to you from the Father, the Spirit of truth who comes from the Father, he will testify on my behalf" (John 15:26). The Spirit of Truth will guide Jesus' disciples to all truth (John 16:13). And, finally, Jesus states, ". . . [I]f I do not go away, the Advocate will not come to you" (John

16:7). In the First Letter of John, Jesus—not the Holy Spirit nor the Spirit of Truth—is declared to be the advocate: ". . . [W]e have an advocate with the Father, Jesus Christ" (1 John 2:1). Other biblical translators often employ counsellor—such as a counsel for the defense in court—comforter, and helper. In Johannine thought, the Spirit of truth who teaches and testifies about Jesus is a gift to his disciples after Jesus disappears from the earth. If Jesus was their advocate before his departure, the Spirit is their comforter and helper now.

Meditation/Journal: Identify one experience of the Holy Spirit you have had as a Paraclete, an Advocate, Truth, Comforter, Helper, Teacher, or Testifier.

Psalm Response: "Show me how you work, GOD; / School me in your ways / Take me by the hand; / Lead me down the path of truth. / You are my Savior, aren't you? / Mark the milestones of your mercy and love, GOD . . . . / From now on every road you travel / Will take you to GOD. / Follow the Covenant signs; / Read the charted directions." (Ps 25: 4–6a, 10)

Pentecost

Scripture: "When the day of Pentecost had come, [the apostles] were all together in one place. And suddenly from heaven there came a sound like the rush of violent wind, and it filled the entire house where they were sitting. Divided tongues, as of fire, appeared among them, and a tongue rested on each of them. All of them were filled with the Holy Spirit and began to speak in other languages, as the Spirit gave them ability. And at this sound the crowd gathered and was bewildered, because each one heard them speaking in the native language of each." (Acts 2:1–4, 6)

Reflection: Pentecost is not a name for nor is it an image of the Holy Spirit. Pentecost is a Jewish celebration on the fiftieth day after Passover; it is called the Feast of Weeks (Exod 34:22; Lev 23:15–21; Deut 16:9–11). The Pentecost presented by the author of Luke-Acts in the CB (NT) Acts of the Apostles is a collection of images gleaned from the HB (OT) indicating the divine presence. The rush of a violent wind is meant to echo the "wind from God" that "swept over the face of the waters" (Gen 1:2) at the beginning of creation. It also recalls Elijah's experience on Mount Horeb (Sinai) (1 Kgs 19:11–12). The fire, another sign of divine presence, recalls the covenant-making ceremony between the LORD and Abram (Gen 15:17), Moses' encounter with God (Exod 3:2), the LORD leading the Israelites (Exod 13:21–22), and God's presence on Mount Horeb (Sinai) (Exod 24:17). The ability of the apostles to speak in other languages and for members of the crowd to understand them reverses the confusion of Babel (Gen 11:1–9); in other words, it (re)creates unity among humankind. The author of Luke-Acts has used the signs of divine presence he found in the HB (OT) and made them signs of the Holy Spirit in the CB (NT). The divine presence is not just outside people, but the divine presence (Holy Spirit) is within them, filling them or connecting to their spirit. However, the author of Luke-Acts has done more than that. Since his theological position is that the Spirit (divine presence) guides everything, he has presupposed Pentecost at the beginning of his gospel. In the nativity material—all unique to Luke's Gospel—everyone is filled with the Holy Spirit; in other words, the author of Luke-Acts presents Pentecost at the beginning of the gospel (Luke 1:15, 35, 41, 67; 2:25–26; 3:16, 22; 4:1) and, parallel, at the beginning of the Acts of the Apostles. Thus, what began biblically as signs (images) of divine presence have been transformed into images (wind, fire, and languages) of the Holy Spirit by the author of Luke-Acts.

While the above account of Pentecost is the one known to most people, there is another version of Pentecost. It is found in John's Gospel on Easter Sunday evening. The risen Johannine Jesus appears to the disciples after passing through locked doors (John 20:19). Pentecost takes places when he breathes on them and says, "Receive the Holy Spirit" (John 20:22). The Johannine author has in mind the second account of creation which features the LORD God breathing the breath of life into the nostrils of the man he created from the dust of the earth, so that the man becomes a living being (Gen 2:7). The Johannine author presents Jesus doing what God did to fulfill the author's Jesus' predictions about the Holy Spirit earlier in the gospel (John 14:16, 26; 15:26; 16:7–15). Thus, in Johannine thought, Jesus breathes the Holy Spirit into his disciples on Easter Sunday evening, while in the Acts of the Apostles, the Spirit comes with a windstorm and pyrotechnics fifty days after Easter.

Meditation/Journal: Using images (metaphors, similes) describe any experience of the Holy Spirit that you have had. Which of the two biblical Pentecosts is your favorite? Why?

Psalm Response: "The God of gods—it's GOD!—speaks out, shouts, 'Earth!' / welcomes the sun in the east, / farwells the disappearing sun in the west. / From the dazzle of Zion, / God blazes into view. / Our God makes his entrance, / he's not shy in his coming. / Starbursts of fireworks precede him. (Ps 50:1–3)

𝔓neuma

Scripture: Jesus said to Nicodemus: "The wind blows where it chooses, and you hear the sound of it, but you do not know where it comes from or where it goes. So it is with everyone who is born of the Spirit." (John 3:8)

Reflection: The Greek noun *pneuma*, which is translated in the above Scripture verse as *wind* and *spirit*, comes from the Greek verb meaning to breathe. Because pneuma can be translated as breath, spirit, or wind, the verb can mean to breathe, to spirit, or to wind. While at first those verbs may seem like nonsense, upon reflection they add a further depth of understanding to Spirit. For example, in the first sentence of the above verse, the Greek can be translated this way: "The spirit blows where it chooses, and you hear the sound of it, but you do not know where it comes from or where it goes." Just like God breathed the divine Spirit into the man at creation (Gen 2:7), so the divine Spirit continues to breeze where it chooses, and we do not know from where it comes or to where it goes. The observation is that the wind can be heard as it passes through tree branches and leaves or as it whistles around buildings, but it cannot be seen. In HB (OT) understanding, the Spirit can be seen as fire and heard as speech (tongues), but no one—except God—knows from where it comes or to where it goes; fire and speech are manifestations of the Spirit—they are not the invisible Spirit. A person born of the Spirit becomes new, divine reality, which is invisible, like the wind. It is like being immersed in a tank of invisible air and breathing deeply.

The Greek noun *pneuma* is the foundation for many nouns in English. For example, *pneumatic* refers to the use of compressed air in tools, machines, and brakes. *Pneumatics* is a branch of physics that deals with the mechanical properties of air. In Christian theology, the study of the Holy Spirit is called *pneumatology*. And any inflammation of the human lungs is called *pneumonia*. Building on *pneuma*'s ambiguous meanings in Greek—breath, spirit, and wind—English uses the Greek word to form numerous

English words—the few above are not exhaustive—indicating breath, wind, or spirit (Spirit).

Meditation/Journal: What other English words do you know built on the Greek noun *pneuma*? What new insight have you received by learning that the Greek word *pneuma* can be translated into English as breath, spirit (Spirit), and wind?

Psalm Response: "Good people, cheer GOD! / Right-living people sound best when praising. / Use guitars to reinforce your Hallelujahs! / Play his praise on a grand piano! / Invent your own new song to him; / give him a trumpet fanfare. / For GOD's Word is solid to the core; / everything he makes is sound inside and out. / The skies were made by GOD's command; / he breathed the word and the stars popped out. / He scooped Sea into his jug, / put Ocean in his keg." (Ps 33: 1–4 6–7)

Pour/Poured (Out)

Scripture: "I [, the LORD,] will pour out my spirit on all flesh . . . . Even on the male and female slaves, in those days, I will pour out my spirit." (Joel 1:28a, 29).

Reflection: Biblically, and in alphabetical and Bible-book order, one can pour (out) anger (Isa 42:25; Jer 7:20; 42:18; 44:6), hot anger (Lam 4:11), ashes (1 Kgs 13:3, 5), bile (Jer 2:11), blood (Lev 8:15; 9:9; Deut 12:27; Pss 79:3, 10; 106:38; Isa 63:6; Zeph 1:17; Matt 26:7; Mark 14:24; Luke 22:20), bowls (Rev 16:2, 3, 4, 8, 10, 12, 17), coins (John 2:15), curse and oath (Dan 9:11), the decreed end (Dan 9:27), deep sleep (Isa 29:10), drink offerings (2 Kgs 16:13; Isa 57:6; Ezek 20:28), entrails (2 Sam 20:10), fury (Lam 2:4), grace (Ps 45:2), groanings (Job 3:24), indignation (Ezek 22:31), libations (Jer 19:13; 32:29; 44:19; Phil 2:17; 2 Tim 4:6), life (Jer 2:12), love (Rom 5:5), lust (Ezek 16:36), oil (Gen 28:18; 35:14; Lev 8:12; 21:10; 1 Sam 10:1; 2 Kgs 9:6; Job 29:6; Ps 92:10; Matt 26:7; Mark 14:3; Luke 10:34), perfume (Song 1:3), prayer (Isa 26:16), rain (Exod 9:33; Judg 5:4; Ps 68:8; Joel 2:23), a river (Rev 12:16), self (Isa 53:12), soul (Job 30:16), water (1 Sam 7:6; 2 Sam 23:16; 1 Chr 11:18; Pss 22:14; 77:17; Mic 1:4; John 13:5; Rev 12:15), wine (Luke 10:34), and wrath (2 Chr 12:7; 34:21, 25; Ezek 20:33, 34; 22:22; 36:18; Nah 1:6; Rev 14:10). The biblical use of pour or poured (out), meaning *to make something flow*, is a metaphorical image (like water being poured from a pitcher into a glass) comparing liquids that can be streamed to other things that can and cannot flow.

In addition to the uses of pour or poured (out) in the previous paragraph, in the above Scripture passage, the prophet Joel presents the LORD declaring that he will pour his spirit on all flesh, even slaves. In his post-Pentecost sermon in the Acts of the Apostles, the Lukan Peter quotes Joel's words (Acts 2:17–18) as predicting and being fulfilled with the event of Pentecost (Acts 2:2–12). Later in the Acts of the Apostles, echoing both Joel and the Acts, the narrator states, "The circumcised believers . . . were astounded that the gift of the Holy Spirit had been poured out even on the Gentiles" (Acts 10:45). The prophet Isaiah notes that in Egypt the LORD poured into princes a spirit of confusion (Isa 19:14), while also stating that justice and righteousness would not exist until a spirit from on high was poured on the land ruined by the Assyrian conquest of Israel and it was transformed into farmland once again (Isa 32:15). In a similar vein, Isaiah portrays the LORD telling Judah, after it was conquered by the Babylonians, that the LORD would pour his spirit upon Jacob's descendants (Isa 44:3b). In the prophet Ezekiel, the Lord GOD declares that he will never again hide his face, when he pours out his spirit upon the house of Israel (Ezek 39:29). In the CB (NT), Paul writes to the Romans about God's love being poured into their hearts through the Holy Spirit (Rom 5:5), and the author of the letter to Titus reminds him that he has been renewed by the Holy Spirit (Titus 3:5), who has been poured out richly through Jesus Christ (Titus 3:6). Thus, employing the metaphorical image of pour/poured (out) biblical authors make the invisible Spirit flow!

Meditation/Journal: Of all the things that can be poured biblically which is your favorite? Explain. In what specific ways has the Spirit made you flow?

Psalm Response: "My heart bursts its banks, / spilling beauty and goodness. / I pour it out in a poem to the king, / shaping the river into words: 'Your throne is God's throne, / ever and always; / And that is why God, your very own God, / poured fragrant oil on your head, / Marking you out as king / from among your dear companions.'" (Ps 45:1, 6a, 7)

Power

Scripture: ". . . [A]s for me [, Micah], I am filled with power, / with the spirit of the LORD, / and with justice and might, / to declare to Jacob his transgression, / and to Israel his sin." (Mic 3:8)

Reflection: Power is the ability or capacity to do something. In the above verse, the HB (OT) prophet Micah tells his readers that he is filled with power, with the Spirit of God, to announce to the northern Kingdom of Israel (Jacob) that its leaders and people have sinned. The political situation that existed when Micah wrote those words was that the Assyrian empire was threatening the northern Kingdom of Israel. Micah, along with other prophets, determined that Assyria's threat was due to Israel's sin, Jacob's lack of following the ways of the LORD. The above verse comes from Micah's second of two judgment speeches in chapter 3. This short speech is addressed to false prophets (Mic 3:5), who had accepted bribes to give favorable prophecies. According to Micah, their words are blocked (Mic 3:6–7), whereas his words are filled with judgment, the gift of authority to indict the leaders and the people of rebellion and sin. Their rebellion comes from the abuse of divinely delegated power (false prophets) by those in both political and religious authority. With his power of the Spirit Micah declares judgment and justice on the whole nation of Israel.

Micah's role, like that of other prophets, was to communicate the LORD's word to his chosen people. God shared his divine power with the prophet he called. That power is given to the apostles in the CB (NT) Acts of the Apostles. The Lukan-Acts narrator recounts John the Baptist's words in Luke's Gospel about Jesus baptizing with the Holy Spirit (Luke 3:16b; Acts 1:5). Then, the Lukan-Acts Jesus instructs his apostles, telling them that they would "receive power when the Holy Spirit [came] upon [them]" (Acts 1:8). It is a power to be Christ's witnesses through teaching, preaching, healing, etc. throughout the known world (Acts 1:8). After his baptism, the Luke-Acts author states that Jesus was full of the Holy Spirit (Luke 4:1), but after his three-fold temptation in the wilderness (Luke 4:1–13), the author states that he is "filled with the power of the Spirit" (Luke 4:14). In other words, he has the ability to teach, preach, heal, etc. In his letter to the Romans, Paul claims for himself similar power as a minister of Christ Jesus to the Gentiles, to whom "by word and deed, by the power of signs and wonders, by the power of the Spirit of God" he has proclaimed the good news (Rom 15:18–19). Earlier in the same letter he had wished the Romans to abound "in hope by the power of the Holy Spirit" (Rom 15:13). In his oldest letter in the CB (NT)—First Letter to the Thessalonians—Paul expresses the idea this way: ". . . [W]e [, Paul, Silvanus, and Timothy,] know . . . that [God] has chosen you, because our message of the gospel came to you not in word only, but also in power and in the Holy Spirit with full conviction" (1 Thess 1:4–5). Thus, just like Micah was filled with power, with the Spirit of God, to announce to the northern Kingdom of Israel (Jacob) that its leaders and people had sinned, so Paul proclaimed the gospel in divine power, in the Holy Spirit, to the Gentiles, who believed him.

Meditation/Journal: Whom have you known who had the capacity to give a speech or to preach truth that affected you deeply? Has the power of the Holy Spirit ever been given to you? Explain.

Psalm Response: "God, the one and only— / I'll wait as long as he says. / Everything I need comes from him, / so why not? / He's solid rock under my feet, / breathing room for my soul. / My help and glory are in God / — granite-strength and safe-harbor-God— / So trust him absolutely, people; / lay your lives on the line for him. / God is a safe place to be. / God said this once and for all; / how many times / Have I heard it repeated? / 'Strength comes / Straight from God.'" (Ps 62:1–2, 7–8, 11)

Pray in the Spirit

Scripture: "Pray in the Spirit at all times in every prayer and supplication. To that end keep alert and always persevere in supplication for all the saints." (Eph 6:18)

Reflection: While prayer is important throughout the CB (NT) letter to the Ephesians (1:15–23; 3:14–21), the above verse represents the only time that the unknown author tells his readers to pray in the Spirit. The letter to the Ephesians is one written in the name of Paul by someone who understood Pauline thought. In his letter to the Romans, Paul tells his readers that the Spirit helps them in their weakness, especially when they do not know how to pray (Rom 8:26). Prayer in the Spirit occurs when the Spirit connects to human spirit. This act of communicating with the transcendent God may include petition, intercession, supplication, confession, praise, and/or thanksgiving. Praying in the Spirit is not a method for compelling God to act, but is the act of the human person opening himself or herself to God and doing his will in his or her life and the lives of all believers (saints).

The author of the short letter of Jude in the CB (NT) also tells his readers to "pray in the Holy Spirit" (Jude 1:20). The Holy Spirit empowers the prayer of Christians. According to Jude, it helps to build on faith (Jude 1:20). Those who do not pray in the Holy Spirit cause division in the community Jude is addressing (Jude 1:19). Coupled with praying in the Spirit is remaining in the love of God, both God's love for people and people's love for God. Both prayer and love in the human person are the result of the Spirit being connected to the spirit. Such a connection is like an electrical current that runs both ways: from people to God and from God to people. The Spirit is like the current carried on the wire from the electricity-generating station to the home; one end of the wire is connected to a person and the other end is connected to God. Prayer in the Spirit flows both ways; love flows both ways. Voiced or silent prayer travels the wire to God, and God's response travels the wire back to the people praying. The love for God travels the wire to God, and God's love for people travels the wire back to people.

Meditation/Journal: What is your definition of prayer in the Spirit? When have you most recently been aware that you were connected to God in prayer in the Spirit? When have you most recently been aware that you were connected to God in love?

Prayer Response: "God can do anything, you know—far more than you could ever imagine or guess or request in your wildest dreams! He does it not by pushing us around but by working within us, his Spirit deeply and gently within us. Glory to God in the church! / Glory to God in the Messiah, in Jesus! / Glory down all the generations! / Glory through all millennia! Oh, yes! (Eph 3:20–21)

Promise of the Father

Scripture: Peter said to the Israelites (Jews): "This Jesus God raised up, and of that all of us are witnesses. Being therefore exalted at the right hand of God, and having received from the Father the promise of the Holy Spirit, he has poured out this that you both see and hear." (Acts 2:32–33)

Reflection: In the Luke-Acts order of events, before Jesus ascends in the Acts of the Apostles, he tells his apostles not to leave Jerusalem, "but to wait there for the promise of the Father" (Acts 1:4a). In Luke's Gospel, before Jesus ascends (the author of Luke-Acts presents an ascension story on Easter Sunday evening at the end of the gospel and another ascension story forty days later in the Acts of the Apostles), he tells his apostles, "I am sending upon you what my Father promised; so stay here in the city until you have been clothed with power from on high" (Luke 24:49). There is no doubt that in the Acts, Jesus is the source of the Spirit received by believers. However, the presupposition of the author is that the Father promised the Spirit to him. A promise is the assurance that something will happen or be done. In his post-Pentecost speech, the Luke-Acts Peter states that Jesus received from the Father the promise of the Holy Spirit, as stated in the above Scripture passage. The pouring out of the Holy Spirit in the events of Pentecost (Acts 2:1–12) is proof, according to the Luke-Acts Peter, that the promise of the Father has been fulfilled through the risen Christ. The dramatic display of wind, fire, and languages are signs that Jesus himself has received the Spirit and shared it with his apostles to inaugurate the reign of God. The only problem is that there is no record of the promise of the Father in the Luke-Acts volumes! Luke may be presuming the reader knows the LORD's promise to pour out his Spirit in the prophet Joel (2:28), which Peter quotes in his post-Pentecost speech (Acts 2:17). The Luke-Acts John the Baptist states that Jesus will baptize with the Holy Spirit (Luke 3:16; Acts 11:16), as does the authors of Matthew's Gospel (3:11), Mark's Gospel (1:8), and John's Gospel (1:33), but none states that it is the Father's promise. Luke may understand the Father's promise as the one made to Abram (Abraham) (Gen 12:3; 18:18; 22:18; 26:4), since Peter refers to Abraham and how all the families of the earth were to be blessed through him (Acts 3:25–26). Peter's (the author of the Acts') phrasing above seems to indicate that the risen Christ received from the Father the promise of the Holy Spirit, which he poured out with visible signs on Pentecost (Acts 2:33). The reader of Luke-Acts is left without a record of the promise of the Father to send the Holy Spirit, but with several possible predictions scattered through his work that the author of Luke-Acts may be considering.

The Father's promise to send the Holy Spirit may be one of those preconceived ideas never critically examined that existed in the milieu of the time without a firm basis in biblical literature. Paul demonstrates that he knows the promise in his letter to the Galatians. After interpreting God's words about all of Abraham's descendants being blessed in him as predicting the conversion of the Gentiles (Gal 3:8), Paul argues that the Gentiles have been redeemed by Christ from the curse of the law (Gal 3:13) so that the blessing of Abraham might come to the Gentiles, and they "might receive the promise of the Spirit through faith" (Gal 3:14). In other words, the promised Spirit is mediated through faith in Christ Jesus, in whom the Gentiles believe. The idea also makes its way in the second-generation Pauline letter to the Ephesians, where it is expressed like it is in Galatians. Paul is presented as writing to believers in Ephesus that after they heard the word about Christ Jesus preached to them, they believed and "were marked with the seal of the promised Holy Spirit" (Eph 1:13). The author of Ephesians may have in mind the words of the prophet Joel (2:28) or even the prophet Ezekiel (36:26–27; 37:14). What seems to have taken place with the idea of the Father's promise of the Holy Spirit is the HB (OT) LORD's promise to send his Spirit was reinterpreted to be the Father's promise to send the Holy Spirit.

Meditation/Journal: Have you received the Father's promise of the Holy Spirit? Explain. To whom do you credit the promise? the fulfillment of it?

Psalm Response: "Into the hovels of the poor, / Into the dark streets where the homeless groan, God speaks: / 'I've had enough; I'm on my way / To heal the ache in the heart of the wretched.' / God's words are pure words, / Pure silver words refined seven times / In the fires of his word-kiln, / Pure on earth as well as in heaven." (Ps 12:5–6)

Q

Quench the Spirit

Scripture: "Do not quench the Spirit. Do not despise the word of prophets." (1 Thess 5:19–20)

Reflection: Long before Paul told the Thessalonians not to quench the Spirit in the CB (NT), HB (OT) and OT (A) authors used the verb mostly, but not exclusively, in reference to fire (Isa 66:24; Jer 17:27; 21:12; Ezek 20:47, 48; Amos 5:6; 2 Esd 16:4, 6; 4 Macc 9:20; 18:20; Heb 11:34) and embers (2 Sam 14:7), tinder (Isa 1:31), burning pitch (Isa 34:10), and coals (4 Macc 9:20); wrath (2 Kgs 22:17; 2 Chr 34:25; Jer 4:4; 7:20; 2 Esd 16:9); and wicks (Isa 42:3; 43:17; Matt 12:20) of lamps (2 Sam 21:17). When it comes to emotions, love cannot be quenched (Song 8:7), neither can passion (Eccl 23:16), but fire-breathing boldness (3 Macc 6:34), deceit (2 Esd 6:27), frenzied desires (4 Macc 3:17), and great emotions (4 Macc 16:4) can be quenched. In the CB (NT), John the Baptist characterizes Jesus as one who will burn chaff with unquenchable fire (Matt 3:12; Luke 3:17), while the Markan Jesus characterizes Gehenna—the Jerusalem garbage dump— as a place of unquenchable fire (Mark 9:43) and where the fire is never quenched (Mark 9:48). In his famous armor-of-God extended metaphor (Eph 6:10–17), the author of the letter to the Ephesians tells his readers to use their shield of faith to quench the evil one's flaming arrows (Eph 6:16).

What Paul has in mind in First Thessalonians is the usual use of water to quench fire. The author of the OT (A) book of Wisdom reflects on the incredible property of water, "which quenches all things" (Wis 16:17), but which God manipulated during the exodus so that "water forgot its fire-quenching nature" (Wis 19:20). Paul, however, emphasizes the fire-like imagery of the Spirit, encouraging the community in Thessalonia not to extinguish the Spirit's fire, not to suppress the Sprit's activity. He also mentions one specific aspect of the Spirit's activity: the work of prophecy, which was manifested with prophetic utterances. Basically, Paul tells the Thessalonians not to pour water on the fire of the Spirit's work within them.

Meditation/Journal: Among the biblical things that can be quenched, what are your three favorites? Why? Have you ever experienced the Spirit being quenched in you? Explain.

Psalm Response: "O my soul, bless GOD! / GOD, my God, how great you are! / beautifully, gloriously robed, / Dressed up in sunshine, / and all heaven stretched out for your tent. / You set earth on a firm foundation / so that nothing can shake it, ever. / You started the springs and rivers, / sent them flowing among the hills. / All the wild animals now drink their fill, / wild donkeys quench their thirst." (Ps 104:1–2, 5, 10–11)

Quiet Spirit

Scripture: ". . . [L]et your adornment be the inner self with the lasting beauty of a gentle and quiet spirit, which is very precious in God's sight." (1 Pet 3:4)

Reflection: The above verse from the CB (NT) First Letter of Peter comes from a section of the letter dealing with household codes of behavior; many of the letters in the CB (NT) have a section devoted to all kinds of human behavior for both males and females. The above verse is from a section addressed to wives, whom the author exhorts to recognize and obey their husbands and not to braid their hair nor wear gold ornaments or fine clothing (1 Pet 3:3). Keeping in mind that this part of the First Letter of Peter was written at a different time in history long removed from our experience, and without missing the kernel of truth that the author presents, the reader—no matter female or male—can discover material upon which to reflect. The author is contrasting shorts, t-shirts, tattoos, and rings—lips, nose, eyebrows, etc.—to the inner, hidden beauty of a follower of Jesus. The inner self is the heart, where were located choice and determination in the ancient world. The quiet spirit is the serene manner of life in which one has a reverent consciousness of God, which informs and dictates one's behavior. The calm and serene spirit are universal Christian values, rather than purely feminine virtues. A quiet spirit is necessary to recognize the connection between human spirit and divine Spirit. Living with a quiet spirit is living in God.

In his First Letter to the Thessalonians, Paul tells Christians "to aspire to live quietly" (1 Thess 4:11), as does the author of the Second Letter to the Thessalonians, who are told to work quietly (2 Thess 3:12). Because modern life is so noisy, distractions are countless. It takes a lot of effort to live with a quiet spirit. The Matthean Jesus described himself as gentle and humble of heart (Matt 11:29). Dare those who follow him forget about a quiet spirit?

Meditation/Journal: How do you quiet your spirit? Where do you quiet your spirit? At what time of the day is it easiest to quiet your spirit? hardest to quiet your spirit?

Psalm Response: [GOD,] I've kept my feet on the ground, / I've cultivated a quiet heart. / Like a baby content in its mother's arms, / my soul is a baby content." (Ps 131:2)

R

Raise the Dead

Scripture: "If the Spirit of him who raised Jesus from the dead dwells in you, he who raised Christ from the dead will give life to your mortal bodies also through his Spirit that dwells in you." (Rom 8:11)

Reflection: God raised Jesus from the dead, and God's Spirit dwells in those who have been baptized into his death (Rom 6:3). After being baptized into Jesus' death, they were buried with him and raised from the dead by the glory of the Father (Rom 6:4). Having the Spirit of Christ is the distinguishing mark of Christian identity. With God's Spirit living within, people are linked to the experience of the risen Christ with a hope for resurrection life. Belonging to the realm of the Spirit sets people free from the bonds of the flesh to partake, ultimately, in the superior world of divine power. Paul states that Jesus Christ "was declared to be Son of God with power according to the spirit of holiness by resurrection from the dead" (Rom 1:4). In other words, the dead body of Jesus was re-inspirited by God, according to Paul, and Jesus was revealed to be the Son of God, the Anointed.

The image of Jesus' dead body being re-inspirited by God is best understood by the author of Luke's Gospel. Jesus is presented as the child conceived by the Spirit (Luke 1:35), making him a Spirit-child. After he has been baptized, the Holy Spirit descends upon him (Luke 3:22), then the same Holy Spirit leads him in the wilderness (Luke 4:1). After making a journey to Jerusalem, he is crucified and, before he dies, his last words entrust his Spirit to the Father (Luke 23:46). Then, God re-inspirited him, raising him from the dead, not with the same physical body, but with a spiritual body (1 Cor 15:44). According to the second volume of Luke-Acts, for forty days Christ instructed his apostles through the Holy Spirit (Acts 1:2) in preparation for the fireworks of Pentecost (Acts 2:1–4). This is where Pauline theology begins. God's Spirit, who raised Jesus from the dead, now dwells in those who have been immersed into his death and resurrection. Like Jesus, those who have been baptized have been raised and are already sharing in new life. The fullness of resurrected life—of the Spirit dwelling in the baptized now—will be given by God when the mortal body dies and the Spirit raises spirit to be joined to Christ in God forever (1 Cor 15:42–49).

Meditation/Journal: In what specific ways do you experience resurrected life—the Spirit dwelling within you—now? What hope does that new life now give you for the future? Explain.

Psalm Response: "May you be blessed by GOD, / by GOD, who made heaven and earth. / The heaven of heavens is for GOD, / but he put us in charge of the earth. / Dead people can't praise GOD— / not a word to be heard from those buried in the ground. / But we bless GOD, oh yes— / we bless him now, we bless him always! / Hallelujah! (Ps 115:15–18)

Revealed through the Spirit

Scripture: ". . . [W]e speak God's wisdom, secret and hidden, which God decreed before the ages for our glory. . . . [A]s it is written, 'What no eye has seen, nor ear heard, / nor the human heart conceived, / what God has prepared for those who love him'—these things God has revealed to us through the Spirit; for the Spirit searches everything, even the depths of God. (1 Cor 2:7, 9–10)

Reflection: The divine wisdom Paul writes about in his CB (NT) First Letter to the Corinthians is hidden in mystery and has existed from the beginning. It's been revealed to Paul, the Corinthians, and all through the Spirit (God) connected to human spirit. Because the Spirit investigates the depths of God while being connected to human spirit, God's wisdom has been revealed to those who follow Jesus, according to Paul. For the sake of salvation (glory), God has chosen to reveal his hidden wisdom to those connected to his Spirit. This divine wisdom is not what the wise (rulers, teachers, etc.) know. This is revelation given by God to the human spirit through God's Spirit. This revelation, according to Paul, is newly disclosed; it reveals something previously hidden in God; God's divine will, God's truth, God's wisdom has been revealed to people by the Spirit.

In the above Scripture passage, Paul quotes what looks like a Bible verse. However, no such verse exists! Paul's quotation is a composition made from Isaiah 52:15bc and 64:3a. Paul may be recalling the verses from memory and thinking that they are connected—at least in his head. The new Pauline verse stresses the newness of the revelation from the Spirit. No human eye has ever seen this spiritual revelation; no human ear has ever heard it spoken before; no human heart could ever have conceived such truth. In other words, no human being could have known the salvation (glory) that God had planned for people who love him. In other words, what was unknown has now been revealed by the Spirit; divine wisdom for which humankind searches has been given by the Spirit, who searches everything, everyone, and even God.

Meditation/Journal: Recently, what has the Spirit revealed to your spirit? Explain. What are your thoughts about Paul's non-biblical quotation?

Psalm Response: GOD, ". . . [Y]ou shaped me first inside, then out; / you formed me in my mother's womb. / I thank you, High God—you're breath-taking! / Body and [spirit], I am marvelously made! / I worship in adoration—what a creation! / You know me inside and out, / you know every bone in my body; / You know exactly how I was made, bit by bit, / how I was sculpted from nothing into something. Like an open book, you watched me grow from conception to birth; / all the stages of my life were spread out before you, / The days of my life all prepared / before I'd even lived one day." (Ps 139:13–16)

Ruah

Scripture: "[The ungodly] reasoned unsoundly, saying to themselves / 'Short and sorrowful is our life, / and there is no remedy when a life comes to its end, / and no one has been known to return from Hades. / For we were born by mere chance, / and hereafter we shall be as though we had never been, / for the breath in our nostrils is smoke, / and reason is a spark kindled by the beating of our hearts; / when it is extinguished, the body will turn to ashes, / and the spirit will dissolve like empty air.'" (Wis 2:1–3)

Reflection: *Rua(c)h* is a Hebrew word meaning *breath, wind, and spirit*. In the above passage from the OT (A) book of Wisdom, the word *ruah* is translated into English as breath, spirit, and air. The author's reflection is a rhetorical device with an imaginary opponent; in the above words, the opponent is the ungodly, who reasons defectively, according to the author.

The opponent thinks that people are born by chance, whereas those who follow God believe that he has a plan. Calling the breath in nostrils smoke flies in the face of God being the animating source of life. Noting that the body disappears like ashes and the spirit like empty air is a statement from a non-believer who thought that life was short, sorrowful, and, since no one was known to have returned from Sheol (the Jewish place where the dead lived) or Hades (the Greek place where the dead lived), confirms for the ungodly that people enter the world by chance and exit it the same way. Reflecting upon the Maccabean account of the death of a mother and her seven sons (2 Macc 7:1–41; 8:3—15:32), the author of the Fourth Book of Maccabees praises the seven, holy youths, who were "moved by an immortal spirit of devotion" (4 Macc 14:6) and agreed to die, while running the course toward immortality (4 Macc 14:4). The seven brothers and their mother stand in opposition to the ungodly in the OT (A) book of Wisdom.

There are no capital letters in Hebrew; therefore, when ruah is translated into English as breath, wind, or spirit, it is up to the translator to decide what English word to use and to decide to capitalize Spirit or leave it spirit. To illustrate this translation problem, here is a passage from the prophet Ezekiel, as it is presented in the New Revised Standard Version (NRSV), with other translation possibilities in fancy brackets: "The hand of the LORD . . . set me down in the middle of a valley; it was full of bones. He said to me, 'Mortal, can these bones live? Prophesy to these bones, and say to them: O dry bones, hear the word of the LORD. Thus says the Lord GOD to these bones: I will cause breath {wind, spirit or Spirit} to enter you, and you shall live. Prophesy to the breath {wind, spirit or Spirit], prophesy, mortal, and say to the breath {wind, spirit or Spirit}: Thus says the Lord GOD: Come from the four winds {breath, spirit or Spirit}, O breath {wind, spirit or Spirit}, and breathe {blow, inspirit} upon these slain, that they may live'" (Ezek 37:1, 3a, 5, 9). The footnotes for this passage in the NRSV indicate that for every time ruah is translated into English, there are several other possibilities, as indicated above. God is a breath, a wind, a spirit (or Spirit), a life force that sustains all living people and things. According to the Bible, God needs nothing to exist; because he exists, we exist. And the way he shares that existence is through his divine breath, wind, and spirit or Spirit.

Meditation/Journal: What do you understand as the ambiguity of the Hebrew word ruah (English: breath, wind, spirit)? In what specific ways do you experience God as breath, as wind, as spirit or Spirit?

Psalm Response: "What a wildly wonderful world, GOD! / You made it all, with Wisdom at your side, / made earth overflow with your wonderful creations. / All the creatures look expectantly to you / to give them their meals on time. / You come, and they gather around; / you open your hand and they eat from it. / If you turned your back, / they'd die in a minute— / Take back your Spirit and they die, / revert to original mud; / Send out your Spirit and they spring to life— / the whole countryside in bloom and blossom." (Ps 140:24, 27–30)

𝕾

𝕾anctifier

Scripture: "Peter, . . . to the exiles, . . . who have been chosen and destined by God the Father and sanctified by the Spirit to be obedient to Jesus Christ and to be sprinkled with his blood: May grace and peace be yours in abundance." (1 Peter 1:1–2)

Reflection: The verb *to sanctify* means *to make holy*, implying that a person has been freed from sin. According to the introduction to the CB (NT) First Letter of Peter, the Father chose those to whom the author is writing and made them holy so they could accept the obligations of those redeemed by Jesus Christ through his death on the cross. The author considers the sprinkling of Jesus' blood to be enacting the second covenant, like Moses' sprinkling blood on the Israelites in the first covenant (Exod 24:8). Peter's readers are told that they, like Israelites in the past, have been elected in accordance with God's plan empowered by the sanctifying power of the Spirit to become the people of the new covenant. This entails, like the old, obedience and sacrifice—Jesus' blood. The Father's choice, according to the author of this letter, is effected by the dynamism of the Spirit.

In his letter to the Romans, Paul writes that the Gentiles have been sanctified by the Spirit (Rom 15:16). Paul's proclamation to the Gentiles results in their transformation to holiness by the Spirit. In his First Letter to the Corinthians, he tells believers in Corinth that they have been washed (baptized), sanctified (made holy), and justified (made acceptable) in the name of Jesus Christ and in the Spirit of God (1 Cor 6:11). In a vein like that of First Peter above, the author of the CB (NT) Second Letter to the Thessalonians tells his readers that God chose them for salvation through sanctification by the Spirit (2 Thess 2:13). In CB (NT) thought, God chooses or elects those Jews and Gentiles who believe that Jesus is his Son, and the Spirit sanctifies them, setting them apart as holy, like God.

Meditation/Journal: In what specific ways has the Spirit sanctified you?

Psalm Response: "Silence is praise to you, / Zion-dwelling God, / And also obedience. / You hear the prayer in it all. / Blessed are the chosen! Blessed the guest / at home in your place! / We expect our fill of good things / in your house, your heavenly manse. / All your salvation wonders / are on display in your trophy room." (Ps 65:1–2, 4–5)

Seal of the Holy Spirit

Scripture: ". . . [I]t is God who establishes us [Paul and Timothy (1 Cor 1:1)] with you [, Corinthians,] in Christ and has anointed us, by putting his seal on us and giving us his Spirit in our hearts as a first installment." (2 Cor 1:21–22)

Reflection: A seal is an authenticating stamp made with wax and a ring or with a raised or engraved sign or emblem that can be pressed into wax to certify a signature or authenticate a document. Modern seals consist of two metal plates, one with raised words or signs and the other with impressed words or signs, which, when squeezed together with paper between the plates, leaves an embossed seal on paper, when the handles mounted to the plates are squeezed together. A seal of wax or crinkled paper confirms authenticity. That is why in the above passage from Paul's Second Letter to the Corinthians in the CB (NT) the apostle, first, makes it very clear that God has established him and Timothy as missionaries with the Corinthians. Then, echoing the baptismal formula, he states that this has occurred in Christ. Also, God has anointed all by putting his authentication mark on them along with the gift of the Spirit as a first installment or down payment with more to follow. The author of the second-generation Pauline letter to the Ephesians tells his readers that they were marked with the seal of the Holy Spirit (Eph 1:13) for the day of redemption (Eph 4:30). Similarly, the Johannine Jesus tells a crowd that God the Father has set his seal on the Son of Man (John 6:27). The Johannine Jesus tells the crowd to work not for physical food but for the food of eternal life, which he, the Son of Man, will give them. God has set his seal—authenticated—Jesus as his Son.

The authentication provided by the seal of the Holy Spirit is like the guarantee presented by Good Housekeeping and the Consumer Product Safety Commission. In 1909, Good Housekeeping created its seal of approval; this meant that a product—appliance, method, recipe, etc.—advertised in the magazine of the same name had been tested by the Good Housekeeping Institute and backed by a two-year limited warranty. In 1962, the seal became a guarantee of the product or its performance. In 1972, the U.S. government created the Consumer Product Safety Commission, which promotes the safety of consumer products by developing safety standards and conducting research into product-related illnesses and injuries. When the USCPSC issues a recall of a product, it sets its seal on it, indicating that it is not safe. Like the seal of the Spirit authenticates the Father's choice of people, the seal of the CPSC authenticates the non-safety of a product for a consumer.

Meditation/Journal: In what specific ways have you experienced the seal of the Spirit?

Psalm Response: "Hallelujah! / Thank GOD! Pray to him by name! / Tell everyone you meet what he has done! / Sing him songs, belt out hymns, / Translate his wonders into music! / Honor his holy name with Hallelujahs, / you who seek GOD. Live a happy life! / Keep your eyes open for GOD, watch for his works, / be alert for signs of his presence. / Remember the world of wonders he has made, / his miracles, and the verdicts he's rendered— / O seed of Abraham, his servant, / O child of Jacob, his chosen." (Ps 105:1–6)

Searcher

Scripture: "The human spirit is the lamp of the LORD, / searching every inmost part." (Prov 20:27)

Reflection: The above proverb comes from the second section of the book of Proverbs (chapters 10 through 22), a collection, according to the author, of Solomon's proverbs. In the HB (OT) book of Proverbs, short sayings, sometimes very loosely connected, follow one after another. The human spirit (or breath) is God's inward light or guide. Like a person shines a flashlight into a dark area to see what is there, Spirit (God) is connected to spirit, and Spirit (God) shines the light everywhere in a human being. Keeping in mind that the Hebrew *ruah* can also mean breath, this proverb means that by connecting Spirit to spirit, God can see and know every nook and cranny where lungs and blood take breath. Not only does God know what is inside a person, but he uses the Spirit he shares with people to search each person's innermost parts. Psychologically, the proverb means that the power to know oneself and articulate it is to share in the LORD's Spirit. The LORD probes thoughts, desires, affections, will, etc. The proverb illustrates the fact that ancient houses did not have windows—because glass had not yet been invented—and the only way to see in the darkness was to light a clay or ceramic lamp, which had a spout at one end for a reed or cloth wick, a hole in the middle into which was poured olive oil, and a handle at the other end. Once the wick was ignited with fire, the house was illumined. Thus, the spirit of the individual person is God's (Spirit's) connective light searching the person's every inner part—every inner room.

It should come as no surprise that Paul uses the basic idea of the proverb in two of his CB (NT) letters. In First Corinthians, he writes "the Spirit searches everything, even the depth of God" (1 Cor 2:10). In his letter to the Romans, Paul applies the idea to prayer. He states that God knows what is in the mind of the Spirit, because the Spirit intercedes for the saints according to God's will (Rom 8:27). The Spirit is a searcher both of God and, when connected to people, of the human spirit. The Spirit (spirit) is like light illuminating dark, hidden places. The Spirit (spirit) is like a group of people with flashlights on a dark night in the woods illuminating trees, bushes, and leaves in the hope of finding a lost person.

Meditation/Journal: In what ways have you experienced the Spirit shining a light on your spirit? What were the results of the searches?

Psalm Response: "By your words I can see where I'm going [, GOD]; / they throw a beam of light on my dark path. / I've committed myself and I'll never turn back / from living by your righteous order. / Everything's falling apart on me, GOD: / put me together again with your Word. / Festoon me with your finest sayings, GOD; / teach me your holy rules. / My life is as close as my own hands, / but I don't forget what you have revealed." (Ps 119:105–109)

Sent

Scripture: Judith sang: "I will sing to my God a new song; / O Lord, you are great and glorious, / wonderful in strength, invincible. / Let all your creatures serve you, / for you spoke, and they were made. / You sent forth your spirit, and it formed them; / there is none that can resist your voice." (Jdt 16:13–14)

Reflection: After a widow named Judith devises and enacts a plan to defeat the enemy of her people, in the OT (A) book named after her, she sings a psalm of thanksgiving to God; two verses from that seventeen-verse song are found in the Scripture text above. She praises God for sending forth his spirit or breath to create all creatures that inhabit the earth. Basically, Judith's victory song credits God with making creatures appear because he sent forth his Spirit to form them. The same idea is expressed by the author of the CB (NT) First Letter of Peter; the writer refers to the Holy Spirit sent from heaven (1 Pet 1:12). His words express the divine origin and initiative of salvation—the subject of the section of the letter (1 Pet 1:10–12).

Whereas God sends the Spirit from heaven to the earth in a three-storied universe cosmology, after Pentecost in the CB (NT) Acts of the Apostles, the Holy Spirit sends missionaries. The author notes that Barnabas and Saul were "sent out by the Holy Spirit" (Acts 13:4) from Antioch to Seleucia. The divine character of Barnabas' and Saul's (Paul's) commission is emphasized. While such direct intervention by the Spirit is characteristic of Luke-Acts, the recurrences are phrased as filled by the Spirit, spoken by the Spirit, or the Spirit fell on, etc. No matter if the Spirit is sent by God or if the Spirit sends others, the message is the same. God causes someone to move from one place to another with his divine presence. The one enabled and sent transmits the divine presence to others.

Psalm Response: "Send out your Spirit [, GOD,] and [all creatures] spring to life— / the whole countryside in bloom and blossom. / The glory of GOD—let it last forever! / Let GOD enjoy his creation! / Oh, let me sing to GOD all my life long, / sing hymns to my God as long as I live. / Oh, let my song please him; / I'm so pleased to be singing to GOD." (Ps 104:30–34)

Spirit

Scripture: Jesus said to a Samaritan woman, "God is spirit, and those who worship him must worship in spirit and truth." (John 4:24).

Reflection: In the CB (NT) Gospel of John, the Johannine Jesus meets a Samaritan woman at a well and begins a lengthy dialogue with her (John 4:1–42). During their discussion about the best place to worship God, Jesus says, ". . . [T]he hour is coming, and is now here, when the true worshipers will worship the Father in spirit and truth, for the Father seeks such as these to worship him" (John 4:23). Then, he adds the above verse. Because God is spirit—even though the prophet Malachi states that both flesh and spirit are his (Mal 2:15b)—God is not tied to a particular place, like Jerusalem or Samaria; in other words, the place for worship is irrelevant. What is relevant, according to the Johannine Jesus, is that people worship in spirit; spirit connects to Spirit, and true worship occurs. While spirit is beyond everything earthly, it is manifested in the Johannine Jesus, who gives the Spirit to those who believe in him. When Spirit finds spirit, an energetic connection is made. In other words, the places where worship occurred have been replaced by Jesus. And those who believe in him discover that they are connected by spirit to him, each other, and the Spirit. Later in John's Gospel, Jesus attends the Festival of Booths (Tabernacles). On the last day of the celebration, he invites people to come to him and drink, for out of him flows the spirit, rivers of living water (John 7:37–38); the image is that of a spring bubbling water to the surface of the earth and forming a flowing river. At the festival, the story about water from the rock (Num 20:2–13) was remembered. After Jesus speaks, the narrator takes over, stating, "Now he said this about the Spirit, which believers in him were to receive, for as yet there was no Spirit, because Jesus was not yet glorified" (John 7:39). In other words, the writer is getting ahead of his own story here! Later in the gospel, after his death and burial Jesus appears to his followers and breathes the Spirit on them (John 20:22). In the scenario created by the Johannine author, the spirit is at work in believers now, and it will be intensified after Jesus' glorification. Like the water from the rock was a blessing from God for his chosen people in the desert, the Johannine Jesus states that the intensified Spirit will be another blessing from God for believers.

In the CB (NT) book of Revelation, the spirit is characterized as seven spirits before God's throne (Rev 1:4; 3:1; 4:5; 5:6). Reference to the sevenfold spirit (Isa 11:2) indicates that the Spirit is perfect; the number seven indicates completeness. The author of Revelation is echoing passages from the HB (OT) book of the prophet Zechariah, who records a vision of a lampstand (menorah) with seven lamps on it (Zech 4:2) and seven eyes of the LORD ranging through the whole earth (Zech 4:10). Revelation 1:4's seven spirits represent God's activity in the world. Revelation 3:1's seven-fold spirit is held by Jesus, while 4:5's seven flaming torches point directly to the Holy Spirit and echo Zech 4:2. Revelation 5:6's seven eyes of the Lamb represent his fullness of knowledge and echo Zech 4:10. Thus, Revelation's seven spirits represent the gift of the Father to his Son and all creation and is often called Spirit or Holy Spirit.

Meditation/Journal: For you, what are the characteristics of true worshipers of the Father in spirit and truth? Make a list. In what specific ways is the Spirit a blessing for you?

Psalm Response: "Sing GOD a brand-new song! / Earth and everyone in it, sing! / Sing to GOD—*worship* GOD! / For GOD is great, and worth a thousand Hallelujahs. / Bring gifts and celebrate, / Bow before the beauty of GOD, / Then to your knees—everyone worship!" (Ps 96:1–2a, 4a, 8–9)

Spirituality 1

Scripture: "So it is with the resurrection of the dead. What is sown is perishable, what is raised is imperishable. It is sown a physical body, it is raised a spiritual body. If there is a physical body, there is also a spiritual body. But it is not the spiritual that is first, but the physical, and then the spiritual." (1 Cor 15:42, 44, 46)

Reflection: In the above passage from Paul's First Letter to the Corinthians in the CB (NT), the apostle uses the image of seed to explain resurrection to his readers. When a tiny seed is planted in the earth, it is physical and perishable; it dies, but a new plant rises from its death. Humans are like the seed; people are physically perishable, but resurrection brings them to new life, imperishability. Like the seed, what is buried is a physical body, but what is raised is an inspirited (spiritual) body. In other words, people are physical first, then they are inspirited (spiritual). The word *spiritual* refers to the inspirited quality of people whose spirits God has connected to the Spirit. Spirituality—formed from Spirit, *al* (meaning *relating to*), and *ity* (meaning *state, condition, quality,* and *identity*)—refers to the quality or condition of being spirit (Spirit); it is the degree of human awareness of the activity of the Spirit in spirit, or, as Paul states, it is having the Spirit of God (1 Cor 7:40). The author of John's Gospel expresses the idea using the language of birth: ". . . [W]hat is born of the Spirit is spirit," states the Johannine Jesus (John 3:6), while in his letter to the Galatians, using the same metaphor as that in First Corinthians, Paul writes, ". . . [I]f you sow to the Spirit, you [your spirit] will reap eternal life from the Spirit (Gal 6:8). Having the Spirit of God connected to human spirit is like a dream in which anything can happen. It is like the experience of being outside yourself looking in or standing beside yourself. Spirituality is like a near-death experience, heading to the light through a birth-canal tunnel only to be called back to life. It is a moment of awareness, ah-ha, transfiguration, worlds opening to each other. We have to search our memories of such experiences in order to draw parallels between them and biblical writers' experiences of Spirit. When Spirit connects to spirit, there is a harmony that ensues, an in-syncness, like a concert where all performers and fans sing the same song together, or like all cell phones vibrating together in an emergency on a university campus, or all football fans in a stadium for the Superbowl, or all baseball fans at a World Series game. In the biblical references that follow, there are multiple biblical attempts to capture in words the experiences of spirituality.

The prophet Isaiah presents God putting his spirit upon his servant (Isa 42:1), echoed by the author of Matthew's Gospel (Matt 12:18). The author of the Second Book of Chronicles prefers to describe the experience of Spirit connecting to spirit as the Spirit of God coming upon one (2 Chr 15:1; 20:14). The prophet Ezekiel writes about the spirit entering him (Ezek 2:2) and how God will put his spirit within his people (Ezek 36:27; 37:14), while the prophet Daniel writes about being endowed by the spirit (Dan 4:8, 9, 18; 5:11) and that a spirit of the gods was in him giving him enlightenment, understanding, and excellent wisdom (Dan 5:14). Ezekiel often writes about the spirit lifting him up and, sometimes, taking him away (Ezek 3:12, 14; 8:3; 11:1, 24; 43:5). In the book of Job, Eliphaz reports that a spirit glided past his face (Job 4:15). The author of Ecclesiastes, asks, "Who knows whether the human spirit goes upward and the spirit of animals goes downward to the earth?" (Eccl 3:21) In the days of Elijah the prophet, the spirit of the LORD was known to carry him away (1 Kgs 18:12; 2 Kgs 2:16), while in the days of Ezekiel's Babylonian Captivity, the spirit of the Lord brought him out (Ezek

37:1). In the CB (NT) Acts of the Apostles, the Lukan Paul says that he is a captive of the Holy Spirit (Acts 20:22), that the Holy Spirit has informed him that imprisonment and persecutions await him (Acts 20:23), and that the Holy Spirit has made some people overseers (shepherds) (Acts 20:28). And just as the spirit can come upon a person, the spirit can depart in death (Sir 38:3; Jas 2:26). This exploration of biblical spirituality is not exhaustive, but it gives an indication of the wealth of ways to express the condition of being spiritual, of having spirit connected to Spirit.

Meditation/Journal: What is your favorite metaphor for expressing your spirituality?

Prayer Response: "How blessed is God! And what a blessing he is! He's the Father of our Master, Jesus Christ, and takes us to high places of blessing in him. Long before he laid down earth's foundations, he had us in mind, had settled on us as the focus of his love, to be made whole and holy by his love. It's in Christ that you, once you heard the truth and believed it (this Message of your salvation), found yourselves home free—signed, sealed, and delivered by the Holy Spirit." (Eph 1:3–4, 13).

Spirituality 2

Scripture: "In the first year of King Cyrus of Persia, . . . the LORD stirred up the spirit of King Cyrus of Persia so that he sent a herald throughout all his kingdom and also declared in a written edict: 'Thus says King Cyrus of Persia: The LORD, the God of heaven, has given me all the kingdoms of the earth, and he has charged me to build him a house at Jerusalem, which is in Judah. Whoever is among you of all his people, may the LORD his God be with him! Let him go up.'" (2 Chr 36:22–23)

Reflection: The Chronicler lived after the Babylonian Captivity ended. The Babylonians were conquered by the Persians, led by Cyrus the Great, whom Isaiah says the LORD summoned (Isa 41:25) and calls shepherd (Isa 44:28), anointed (Isa 45:1), and builder (Isa 45:13). The HB (OT) book of Ezra and the OT (A) book of First Esdras also state that the LORD stirred the spirit of King Cyrus of Persia (Ezra 1:1; 1 Esd 2:2), along with the heads of the families of Judah and Benjamin, priests, Levites, and everyone else (Ezra 1:5; 1 Esd 2:8). Among others whose spirit God stirred are Kings Pul and Tilgath-pilneser of Assyria (1 Chr 5:26), Samson (Judg 13:25), Susanna

(Sus 1:45 [Dan 13:45]), the kings of the Medes (Jer 51:11), and the spirit of Zerubbabel, governor of Judah, and the spirit of Joshua son of Jehozadak, the high priest, and the spirit of all the remnant of the people (Hag 1:14). The image of the LORD stirring the spirit connotes rousing someone to action, like one moves a spoon or other instrument through a liquid in order to mix it. Being stirred by the LORD is an aspect of spirituality, as noted above. Being stirred by the LORD is another way to refer to the inspired quality of people whose spirits God has connected to the Spirit. Spirituality—formed from Spirit, *al* (meaning *relating to*), and *ity* (meaning *state, condition, quality,* and *identity*)—refers to the quality or condition of being spirit (Spirit); it is the degree of human awareness of the activity of the Spirit in spirit.

Besides being stirred, biblical spirit can be shared, such as when God takes spirit from Moses and puts on seventy elders (Num 11:17); the spirit rested on them (Num 11:25, 26), just like the Holy Spirit rested upon Simeon (Luke 2:25). Biblical spirit can come upon one, like it came upon Othniel (Judg 3:10), Jephthah (Judg 11:29), Saul (1 Sam 11:6; 19:23), David (1 Sam 16:14), Saul's messengers (1 Sam 19:20), and Mary (Luke 1:35). The spirit rushed on Samson (Judg 14:6; 15:14), while it fell upon Ezekiel (Ezek 11:5) and all hearing the word (Acts 10:44; 11:15). The spirit took possession of Gideon (Judg 6:34), was the agent of revelation and guide for Simeon (Luke 2:26, 27), and, as reported by Ezekiel, led the four living creatures (Ezek 1:12, 20). All those images are attempts to capture in words experiences of the spirit being connected to Spirit. As noted above, we have to search our memories of such experiences in order to draw parallels between them and biblical writers' experiences of Spirit. When Spirit connects to spirit, there is a harmony that ensues, an in-syncness, that rouses someone to action and spreads, rests, comes upon, rushes, and falls upon others.

Meditation/Journal: From all the metaphors listed above, what is your favorite metaphor for expressing your spirituality?

Psalm Response: "Be glad, Zion Mountain; / Dance, Judah's daughters! / [God] does what he said he'd do! / Circle Zion, take her measure, / count her fortress peaks, / Gaze long at her sloping bulwark, / climb her citadel heights— / Then you can tell the next generation / detail by detail the story of God, / Our God forever, / who guides us till the end of time." (Ps 48:11–14)

T

Temple

Scripture: "Do you not know that you are God's temple and that God's Spirit dwells in you? If anyone destroys God's temple, God will destroy that person. For God's temple is holy, and you are that temple." (1 Cor 3:16–17)

Reflection: In his First Letter to the Corinthians in the CB (NT), Paul tells the Corinthian community that it, collectively, is God's temple in which dwells the Spirit. Paul has in mind the Jerusalem Temple or any other such building in which a god or goddess was believed to live. While a statue of the god or goddess usually was found in a temple, the Israelites believed that the LORD lived in the Jerusalem Temple, seated on the mercy seat, the cover of the box containing the tablets of the covenant. Using the basic idea of a temple as a dwelling place for God, Paul names the Corinthian community as the dwelling place for God's Spirit. Later, in the same letter, the apostle asks, ". . . [D]o you not know that your body is a temple of the Holy Spirit within, which you have from God, and that you are not your own?" (1 Cor 6:19) What Paul says about the community above, is transferred to the individual. The Spirit defines existence in the body as existence before God. Spirit is connected to spirit. Thus, the Spirit is present both collectively and individually; the body—collectively and individually—is the place where the Spirit dwells. In other words, in Pauline thought, the body—collectively and individually—is a moving, walking-around temple!

In his dialogue with the Samaritan woman, the Johannine Jesus states that God cannot be tied to a particular place or a particular building because "God is spirit, and those who worship him must worship in spirit and truth" (John 4:24). Again, Spirit connects to spirit; no specific building is necessary. The author of the CB (NT) First Letter of Peter invites his readers to come to Christ, "a living stone, though rejected by mortals yet chosen and precious in God's sight, and like living stones, [to] let [them]selves be built into a spiritual house, to be a holy priesthood, and to offer spiritual sacrifices acceptable to God through Jesus Christ" (1 Pet 2:4–5). This is the only place in the Bible where the risen Christ is referred to as a living stone, more accurately a dressed stone suitable for building. Just as Jesus was rejected, some of Peter's readers are being rejected. Nevertheless, they are being built into a living house of Spirit, a temple, a dwelling place for God's Spirit. God is building a new temple (collectively) out of individual people in which holiness dwells: the Spirit, the priesthood, and sacrifices.

Meditation/Journal: In what specific ways are you a temple, a dwelling place for God's Spirit? In what specific ways are those with whom you live temples, dwelling places for God's Spirit?

Psalm Response: "What a beautiful home, GOD-of-the-Angel-Armies! / I've always longed to live in a place like this, / Always dreamed of a room in your house, / where I could sing for joy to God-alive! / And how blessed all those in whom you live, / whose lives become roads you travel . . . . / One day spent in your house, this beautiful place of worship, / beats thousands spent on Greek island beaches." (Ps 84:1–2, 5, 10)

Tongues

Scripture: ". . . [T]hose who speak in a tongue do not speak to other people but to God; for nobody understands them, since they are speaking mysteries in the Spirit." (1 Cor 14:2)

Reflection: Speaking in tongues, called glossolalia, while considered a manifestation of the Spirit for the common good by Paul (1 Cor 12:7, 10), is the act of speaking in a language incomprehensible to the speaker and those hearing it. In his discussion of this spiritual gift, Paul does not consider those speaking in tongues doing so to others, but to God, who alone understands them. That is why the apostle writes that various kinds of tongues need the gift of the interpretation of tongues (1 Cor 12:10). Tongues are a sign for unbelievers, Paul tells the Corinthians (1 Cor 14:22), but he also thinks they need to be interpreted for unbelievers and believers alike. He makes his point in question form: "If . . . the whole church comes together and all speak in tongues, and outsiders or unbelievers enter, will they not say that you are out of your mind?" (1 Cor 14:23) This manifestation of the Spirit requires the power to interpret (1 Cor 14:13). Speaking in tongues is not to be forbidden, according to Paul (1 Cor 14:39), but interpretation is required to maintain order in the community.

Speaking in tongues appears frequently in the CB (NT) Acts of the Apostles. It begins with the experience of Pentecost, when all gathered are filled with the Holy Spirit and begin to speak in other languages, as the Spirit gives them the ability (Acts 2:4). As each individual hears his or her native language spoken, the confusion of Babel is reversed (Gen 11:1–9). Through the Spirit, those who had once been scattered because of the lack of understanding each other's languages are united. That experience is repeated when Peter visits the home of the Gentile Cornelius and, while speaking, he hears Cornelius and his household speaking in tongues (Acts 10:46). In Ephesus, Lukan Paul lays his hands on a group of twelve believers, the Holy Spirit comes upon them, and they speak in tongues (Acts 19:6). Thus, Paul in his First Letter to the Corinthians and the author of the Acts of the Apostles express the potential value of glossolalia and its dangers.

Meditation/Journal: What has been your experience of speaking in tongues? of hearing others speak in tongues?

Psalm Response: "Turn your back on evil, / work for the good and don't quit. / GOD loves this kind of thing, / never turns away from his friends. / Live this way and you've got it made, / but bad eggs will be tossed out. / The good get planted on good land / and put down healthy roots. / Righteous chews on wisdom like a dog on a bone, / rolls virtue around on his tongue. / His heart pumps God's Word like blood through his veins; / his feet are as sure as a cat's." (Ps 37:27–31)

Spirit of Truth

Scripture: Jesus said: "I still have many things to say to you, but you cannot hear them now. When the Spirit of truth comes, he will guide you into all the truth; for he will not speak on his own, but will speak whatever he hears, and he will declare to you the things that are to come." (John 16:12–13)

Reflection: The unique phrase *the Spirit of truth* is found only in Johannine literature (John's Gospel and 1 John). In the CB (NT) Gospel of John, the Spirit of truth is identified as the Paraclete (Advocate) (John 14:16–17). The phrase refers to God's reliability. The Gospel of John is designed to expose the truth of God, revealed by Jesus, who is himself the truth (John 14:6). The Spirit of truth, according to the Johannine Jesus, comes from the Father, but is sent by Jesus (John 15:26). Earlier in John's Gospel, Jesus told his disciples that he would ask the Father to give them the Spirit of truth to be with them forever (John 14:16–17). The Spirit of truth in Johannine thought bears witness to Jesus; that is why the Spirit of truth is not given during Jesus' earthly life (John 7:39). After Jesus' death and resurrection, the Spirit of truth, according to the above Scripture passage, will guide believers to all truth.

This role of the Spirit of truth is illustrated in the CB (NT) First Letter of John. The author writes, "Whoever knows God listens to us, and who ever is not from God does not listen to us. From this we know the spirit of truth and the spirit of error" (1 John 4:6bc). In other words, those who listen to the proclaimed word know the spirit of truth. The reliability of God is disclosed by those hearing the word proclaimed to them. The Spirit witnesses to the identity of the Son of God and the historical Jesus. The community of Christ is where the spirit of truth reigns, but false teachers bring the spirit of error, according to the polemic against false teachers in the First Letter of John. Within the Johannine circle is found the Spirit of God, the Spirit of Truth. Jesus came by water and blood, according to the letter, "And the Spirit is the one that testifies, for the Spirit is the truth" (1 John 5:6).

Meditation/Journal: In what specific ways has the Spirit of truth guided you to truth? In what specific ways has God revealed his reliability to you?

Psalm Response: "Train me, GOD, to walk straight; / then I'll follow your true path / Put me together, one heart and mind; / then, undivided, I'll worship in joyful fear. / From the bottom of my heart I thank you, dear Lord; / I've never kept secret what you're up to. / You've always been great toward me—what love! (Ps 86:11–13a)

U

Unction

Scripture: ". . . Samuel took the horn of oil, and anointed [David] in the presence of his brothers; and the spirit of the LORD came mightily upon David from that day forward." (1 Sam 16:13a)

Reflection: Before Samuel anointed David, he had anointed Saul (1 Sam 10:1), whom he told that the spirit of the LORD would possess (1 Sam 10:6). In both accounts of the anointing of David and Saul, oil is a sign of the LORD's Spirit. The word unction—coming from the Latin verb *un-guere*, meaning *to smear* or *to anoint*—means *to anoint with oil* or *to rub oil* on someone. Usually olive oil was poured on the head of the king being anointed; however in the HB (OT) both persons (priests, kings, etc.) and things (altar, vestments, etc.) were anointed. When someone was anointed, he was set apart, consecrated by God's Spirit. "The spirit of the Lord GOD is upon me," states the prophet Isaiah, "because the LORD has anointed me" (Isa 61:1). In his first major discourse (sermon, homily), the Lukan Jesus, who is "filled with the power of the Spirit" (Luke 4:14), begins with Isaiah's text (Luke 4:18), then declares that it is being fulfilled in the hearing of those present (Luke 4:21). Keeping in mind that the author of Luke's Gospel is the same author of the Acts of the Apostles, "Jesus, whom [the Lord] anointed" (Acts 4:27), is described by Peter to Cornelius as Jesus of Nazareth, anointed by God with the Holy Spirit (Acts 10:38).

In Mark's Gospel, the earliest of the four gospels, it is an unnamed woman, who came into the house, while Jesus was eating, "with an alabaster jar of very costly ointment of nard, and . . . broke open the jar and poured the ointment on his head" (Mark 14:8; Matt 26:7). In other words, a woman anoints the Anointed One; however, the evangelist has toned down the explosive quality of the woman's action by portraying Jesus saying that she anointed his body beforehand for burial (Mark 14:8; Matt 26:12). Because the author of Luke's Gospel has already identified Jesus as God's Anointed One, the unnamed woman anoints Jesus' feet (Luke 7:37–38), while in John's Gospel, it is Mary—sister of Martha and Lazarus—who anoints Jesus' feet (John 12:3). In the fourth gospel, Andrew tells his brother, Simon (Peter), "We have found the Messiah," after which the narrator declares, "which is translated Anointed" (John 1:41). In other words, the Hebrew word *Messiah* means *Anointed*, just like the Greek word *Christ* means *Anointed*. In the First Letter of John, anointing becomes a mark of new life. The author tells his readers that they have been anointed by the Holy One" (God) (1 John 2:20). That anointing abides in them and teaches them all things (1 John 2:27); that anointing is the Spirit. Paul makes this clear in his Second Letter to the Corinthians: ". . . God who establishes us with you in Christ . . . has anointed us, by . . . giving us his Spirit in our hearts . . ." (2 Cor 1:21–22). Thus, one sign of the Spirit is unction, being anointed with oil on the head. This occurs in baptism, confirmation, and the ordination of priests (on the hands) and bishops (on the head).

Meditation/Journal: When have you been anointed? Did you receive the Holy Spirit? If you have never been anointed with olive oil, in what specific ways has God given you the Spirit?

Psalm Response: "My heart bursts its banks, / spilling beauty and goodness. / I pour it out in a poem to the king, / shaping the river into words: Your throne is God's throne, / ever and always . . . . You love the right / and hate the wrong. / And that is why God, your very own God, / poured fragrant oil on your head, / Marking you out as king / from among your dear companions." (Ps 45:1, 6a, 7)

Spirit of Understanding

Scripture: "A shoot shall come out from the stump of Jesse, / and a branch shall grow out of its roots. / The spirit of the LORD shall rest on him, the spirit of . . . understanding . . . ." (Isa 11:1–2ab)

Reflection: In the above Scripture passage, God promises a new king in David's line; David's father was Jesse. The passage may be a critique of the then-current king, Ahaz, but the focus here is on the spirit of understanding that will rest on the new king, just like the spirit came mightily upon David after Samuel anointed him (1 Sam 16:13). The spirit of the LORD is the source for the king's understanding—his ability to plan wisely and be a great military leader. Understanding is the ability to grasp the meaning of something, insight, the ability to interpret in a particular way. Understanding is the gift of grasping the Spirit-spirit connection; it is spiritual understanding. The author of the second-generation, Pauline letter to the Colossians calls it being filled with knowledge of God's will in spiritual understanding (Col 1:9). Job's friend, Elihu, states, ". . . [I]t is the spirit in a mortal, the breath of the Almighty, that makes for understanding" (Job 32:8), while the author of the HB (OT) book of Proverbs declares, ". . . [O]ne who is cool in spirit has understanding" (Prov 17:27b). The LORD's, the everlasting God's, understanding is unsearchable (Is 40:28); the Spirit of the LORD connects to human spirit and gives understanding to mere mortals.

The prophet Daniel is given as one who illustrates that point. Daniel is known as one "who is endowed with a spirit of the holy gods" (Dan 5:11); he has "an excellent spirit . . . and understanding to interpret dreams, explain riddles, and solve problems" (Dan 5:12). Indeed, "the spirit of the gods" was in him, and understanding was found in him (Dan 5:14). Daniel fulfills OT (A) Sirach's words: "If the great Lord is willing, / he will be filled with the spirit of understanding" (Sir 39:6a). Jesus, who is characterized by the author of Luke-Acts as filled with the Spirit, gives instructions through the Holy Spirit to the apostles over a forty-day period (Acts 1:2). In other words, he enables them to grasp the meaning of his teaching and to interpret it as spiritual understanding.

Meditation/Journal: In what specific ways is the spirit of understanding manifested in your life?

Psalm Response: "I grasp and cling to whatever you tell me; / GOD, don't let me down! / I'll run the course you lay out for me / if you'll just show me how. / Give me insight so I can do what you tell me— / my whole life one long, obedient response. / With your very own hands you formed me; / now breathe your wisdom over me so I can understand you. / With your instruction, I understand life . . . . I'm your servant—help me understand what that means, / the inner meaning of your instructions. / The way you tell me to live is always right; / help me understand it so I can live to the fullest." (Ps 119:31–32, 34, 73, 104a, 125, 144)

Unity

Scripture: "I took two staffs, one I named Favor, the other I named Unity, and I tended the sheep. I took my staff Favor and broke it, annulling the covenant that I had made with all the peoples. Then I broke my second staff Unity, annulling the family ties between Judah and Israel." (Zech 11:7b, 10, 14)

Reflection: The HB (OT) prophet Zechariah satirizes the corrupt leaders of Judah by telling a parable about becoming a shepherd at the LORD's request (Zech 11:4–7a). While the two staffs represent the goals of the good shepherd of the sheep, the prophet breaks them, indicating that the people are in a time of trouble and conflict. He abandons all hope for the reunion of the Northern Kingdom of Israel and the Southern Kingdon of Judah, both of which traced their origin (unity) to a single ancestor, Jacob. In other words, the prophet Zechariah demonstrates disunity by his action of breaking the staff named Unity.

With disunity in mind, the writers of the CB (NT) focus on unity brought about by the Spirit. The author of the second-generation Pauline letter to the Ephesians tells his readers to make "every effort to maintain the unity of the Spirit in the bond of peace" because "[t]here is one body and one Spirit, just as you were called to the one hope of your calling" (Eph 4:3–4). The author's hope is that all his readers will come "to the unity of the faith" (Eph 4:13). In a similar vein, the author of the First Letter of Peter tells his readers to "have unity of spirit" (1 Pet 3:8). Paul refers to unity as "any sharing in the Spirit" in his letter to the Philippians (2:1), as does the author of the mis-named letter to the Hebrews (6:4). The disunity that had plagued the Jews is turned to unity through the Spirit by followers of Jesus.

Meditation/Journal: In your world, where do you find disunity? Where do you find unity? In what specific experiences do you discover the Spirit bringing about the unity of human spirits?

Psalm Response: "How wonderful, how beautiful, / when brothers and sisters get along! / It's like costly anointing oil / flowing down head and beard, / Flowing down Aaron's beard / flowing down the collar of his priestly robes. / It's like the dew on Mount Hermon / flowing down the slopes of Zion. / Yes, that's where GOD commands the blessing, / ordains eternal life." (Ps 133:1–3)

𝔙

𝔙oice

Scripture: "The oracle of David, son of Jesse, / the oracle of the man whom God exalted, / the anointed of the God of Jacob, / the favorite of the Strong One of Israel: The spirit of the LORD speaks through me, / his word is upon my tongue." (2 Sam 23:1b–2).

Reflection: In the second to last chapter of the HB (OT) Second Book of Samuel, some last words of a Davidic poet appear. After the author identifies himself, he states that the spirit of the LORD speaks through him, when he speaks. The Markan Jesus alludes to the Holy Spirit speaking through King David, when quoting Psalm 110:1 (Mark 12:36). Likewise, the author of the Second Letter of Peter states that "men and women moved by the Holy Spirit spoke from God" (2 Pet 1:21). Privately, the Markan Jesus tells Peter, James, John, and Andrew that they will be persecuted for proclaiming the good news, but they should not worry "beforehand about what [they] are to say, but to say whatever is given [them] at that time, for it is not [they] who speak, but the Holy Spirit" (Mark 13:11). The Matthean Jesus tells the missionary twelve basically the same; however he adds that it is the Spirit of their Father speaking through them (Matt 10:20). Because of the role of the Spirit, and because in Mark's Gospel the scribes think that Jesus is casting out demons with the power of Beelzebul (Mark 3:22), the Markan Jesus declares that such a claim is an insult to the Holy Spirit that it can never be forgiven (Mark 3:29). The author of Matthew's Gospel presents Jesus casting out demons by the Spirit of God (Matt 12:28)—as does the author of Luke's Gospel (11:20)—before declaring that people who blaspheme against the Spirit will not be forgiven (Matt 12:32). The author of Luke's Gospel provides a different setting for the saying (Luke 12:10). Such testing or insulting the Spirit is often phrased as testing the LORD or testing God in the HB (OT) (Exod 17:2, 7; Deut 6:16); the Lukan Jesus quotes Deuteronomy 6:16 during his three-fold temptation scene (Luke 4:12). While putting God to the test is used in the CB (NT) Acts of the Apostles (15:10), the author—the same as that of Luke's Gospel—often refers to it as lying to the Holy Spirit (Acts 5:3) or putting the Spirit of the Lord to the test (Act 5:9). In his long speech recounting HB (OT) history, Stephen refers to the act as opposing the Holy Spirit (Act 7:51).

Nevertheless, throughout the Acts of the Apostles the Spirit speaks. In the author's narration of the events of Pentecost, those gathered are filled with the Holy Spirit and prompted to speak in other languages as the Spirit gave them the ability to do so (Acts 2:4). The Spirit speaks to Peter (10:19), to Barnabas, Simeon (Niger), Lucius, Manaen, and Saul (Acts 13:2), forbids Paul and Timothy from speaking the word in Asia (Acts 16:6) and from going to Bithynia (Acts 16:7), and prompts the prophet Agabus to deliver the Holy Spirit's words to Paul and his companions (Acts 21:4, 11). In Rome, Lukan Paul declares that the Holy Spirit was right in what he said through the prophet Isaiah (Acts 28:25), thus claiming inspiration for Isaiah 6:9–10 (Acts 28:26–27). Similarly, the author of the CB (NT) Letter to the Hebrews claims that the Holy Spirit speaks (Heb 3:7) in Psalm 95:7–11 (Heb 3:7–11) and testifies (Heb 10:15) in Jeremiah 31:31–34 (Heb 10:16–17). In his First Letter to the Corinthians, Paul claims inspiration for those who say "Jesus is Lord," while denying inspiration for those who state, "Let Jesus be cursed!" (1 Cor 12:3) Not to be forgotten is the claim of the author of the CB (NT) book of Revelation; repeatedly, he urges his readers to "listen to what the

Spirit is saying to the churches" (Rev 2:7a, 11a, 17a, 29; 3:6, 13, 22). Later in the book, he records the Spirit saying, "Yes, [those who die in the Lord] will rest from their labors, for their deeds follow them" (Rev 14:13b), and "The Spirit and the bride say, 'Come'" (Rev 22:17a). Thus, the Spirit has a voice. Biblically, he speaks through people and in Scripture. Those who blaspheme or insult the Spirit are guilty of an unforgivable sin. And the final words about the Spirit's voice are about listening to what he says to communities spread around the Mediterranean Sea.

Meditation/Journal: In what specific ways has the Spirit spoken to you? Through whom have you heard the Spirit speak? Explain.

Psalm Response: "GOD thunders across the waters, / Brilliant, his voice and his face, streaming brightness— / GOD across the flood waters. / GOD's thunder tympanic, / GOD's thunder symphonic. / GOD's thunder smashes cedars, / GOD topples the northern cedars. / GOD's thunder spits fire. / GOD thunders, the wilderness quakes . . . . / GOD's thunder sets the oak trees dancing / A wild dance, whirling; the pelting rain strip their branches. / We fall to our knees—we call out, 'Glory!'" (Ps 29:3–5, 7–8a, 9)

𝔚

𝔚ater

Scripture: "Jesus answered [the woman of Samaria], 'If you knew the gift of God, and who it is that is saying to you, "Give me a drink," you would have asked him, and he would have given you living water.'" (John 4:10)

Reflection: The image of water for the Spirit is strewed throughout biblical literature. The Johannine Jesus' request of a drink from a Samaritan woman at Jacob's well prompts a dialogue about living or spring water, which originally referred to the LORD and the salvation that comes from him (Jer 2:13; Sir 24:21b). However, in John's Gospel, a drink of water functions as baptism in living water. The passage is built on the prophet Isaiah's invitation to "everyone who thirsts" to "come to the waters" (Isa 55:1). The woman asks Jesus, "Where do you get that living water?" (John 4:11b) In his vision of the future "living waters" flowing "out from Jerusalem" (Zech 14:8)—a reference to the Gihon spring with abundant water—the author of John's Gospel presents his Jesus stating to the Samaritan woman, "The water that I will give will become . . . a spring of water gushing to eternal life" (John 4:14b). The bubbling, life-giving spring not only echoes Proverbs 18:4, but reminds the reader of the Israelites' words to Moses—"Give us water to drink" (Exod 17:2)—and the act of Moses striking a rock and water gushing out for the people to drink (Exod 17:5–6). Paul reminds his readers that it was spiritual (of the Spirit) drink consumed by the Israelites (1 Cor 10:4). In other words, whoever is led to God by Jesus through his Spirit becomes a spring, a bearer of salvation for others, which is what the Samaritan woman becomes (John 4:29, 39–42). To fully understand the connection between water and Spirit, the reader must go back to the previous Johannine dialogue between Jesus and Nicodemus (John 3:1–15). Jesus tells the Pharisee that he must be "born of water and Spirit" (John 3:5), because "what is born of the Spirit is spirit" (John 3:6). The vehicle for Spirit to connect to spirit is water (baptism). Later, in Johannine literature, the author of the First Letter of John writes about Jesus who came by water and Spirit (1 John 5:6–8). All the Johannine dialogues about water reach a crescendo at the end of Jesus' attendance at the Festival of Booths, when he, echoing biblical passages above, states, "Let anyone who is thirsty come to me, and let the one who believes in me drink. As the scripture has said, 'Out of the believer's heart shall flow rivers of living water'" (John 7:37b–38). The narrator quickly adds that Jesus was speaking about the Spirit, but as of the timeline of the gospel, was not yet existent, because Jesus had not yet been glorified (risen) from the dead (John 7:39); that will take place later in John (20:22).

The image of water (baptism) for Spirit in the CB (NT) also occurs in Paul's First Letter to the Corinthians. After reminding the Corinthians of what they used to be, Paul tells them that they were washed in the name of the Lord Jesus Christ and in the Spirit of God (1 Cor 6:11). In the same letter, he reminds them that it was in one Spirit that they were all baptized into one body and made to drink of one Spirit (1 Cor 12:13). As noted above, a drink of water functions as baptism in living water or eternal life. The author of the Letter to Titus states that God, according to his mercy, saved the letter's readers through the water of rebirth (echoing the Johannine dialogue between Jesus and Nicodemus) and renewal by the Holy Spirit (Titus 3:5). In a similar vein, the author of the CB (NT) book of Revelation writes that he heard a voice from the one seated on a throne (God), state, "To the thirsty I will give water as a gift from the spring of the water of life" (Rev 21:6c). Before this, the author sees "the water of life, bright as crystal, flowing from the throne of God" (Rev 22:1). The previous words are restated by the author: ". . . [L]et everyone who is thirsty come. / Let anyone who wishes take the water of life as a gift" (Rev 22:17cd)—echoing Isaiah 55:1. Thus, the gift of God is living water (Spirit), which people are invited to drink spiritually; it gushes or bubbles to eternal life. In other words, through water Spirit connects to spirit.

Meditation/Journal: In what specific ways have you experienced the Spirit as living water or eternal life? In what specific ways have you accepted the invitation to partake of spiritual drink?

Psalm Response: "God—you're my God! / I can't get enough of you! / I've worked up such hunger and thirst for God, / traveling across dry and weary deserts. / So here I am in the place of worship, eyes open, / drinking in your strength and glory. / In your generous love I am really living at last! / My lips brim praises like fountains. / I bless you every time I take a breath; / My arms wave like banners of praise to you." (Ps 63:1–4)

𝔚eigh the Spirit

Scripture: "All one's ways may be pure in one's own eyes, / but the LORD weighs the spirit." (Prov 16:2)

Reflection: The first verse of chapter 16 of the HB (OT) book of Proverbs is about the heart being the organ of planning and the tongue being the organ of speaking and execution of human plans. However, in a world created and controlled by God, people do not have the power to put their plans into effect or to control their course. Thus, a person's ways or plans may be considered correct in his or her own eyes, but the LORD weighs the spirit; in other words, the author of Proverbs thinks that God evaluates their importance or the intention of the plan-maker. Because Spirit and spirit are immaterial, they cannot be weighed on a scale, but the Spirit connected to human spirit gives God the opportunity to know what a person intends.

Chapter 16 of Proverbs occurs in the middle of a section of proverbs attributed to Solomon (Prov 10:1—22:16). Because human wisdom is limited in scope, in the Israelite world it must submit to God, who alone can bring successful—and even unimaginable—results. Thus, only God can plumb the depths of the human heart and its plans. So, for the successful outcome of plans, a person must trust God, which God recognizes when Spirit connects to spirit.

Meditation/Journal: What most recent plan of yours was successful because God, whom you trust, weighed your spirit and found it pure?

Psalm Response: "GOD answer you on the day you crash, / The name God-of-Jacob put you out of harm's reach, / Send reinforcements from Holy Hill, / Dispatch from Zion fresh supplies. / Give you what your heart desires, / Accomplish your plans. / When you win, we plan to raise the roof / and lead the parade with our banners. / May all your wishes come true!" (Ps 20:1–2, 4–5)

Wind

Scripture: "In the beginning when God created the heavens and the earth, the earth was a formless void and darkness covered the face of the deep, while a wind from God swept over the face of the waters" (Gen 1:1–2).

Reflection: Because the Hebrew word for wind, breath, and spirit is *ruah*, the "wind from God" in the above Scripture passage can also be translated "spirit of God" or "breath of God." The wind, spirit, or breath is life. *Ruah* gives life to everything and everyone that God creates. In the CB (NT), the author of the Acts of the Apostles—the same author of Luke's Gospel— echoes the triple meaning of *ruah* by using the Greek word *pneuma*, which can mean wind, breath, and spirit. On the day of Pentecost, the author states, ". . . [S]uddenly from heaven there came a sound like the rush of a violent wind . . ." (Acts 2:2). The verse could also be translated as "a sound like the rush of a violent breath" or "a sound like the rush of a violent spirit." The oxymorons *violent breath* and *violent spirit* open the narrative about Pentecost to further reflection.

The image of wind for the Spirit is found in the last of eight visions found in the prophet Zechariah. He sees four chariots and asks the angel who speaks with him the meaning of the four chariots. The angel—God in disguise—states, "These are the four winds of heaven going out, after presenting themselves before the Lord of all the earth" (Zech 6:5). "The four winds" could also be translated into English as "the four spirits" or "the four breaths." The four winds (spirits, breaths) represent the four cardinal directions: North, South, East, and West. They represent the totality of the earth, and the four winds (spirits, breaths) represent God's heavenly patrol assigned to watch over the world's affairs. Later in the vision, the angel informs the prophet that the patrol to the north country has set God's spirit at rest in the north country (Zech 6:8); this establishes Judah's security, since it was from the north that Judah's enemies came, and it was from the north that Judah's Babylonian exiles returned from captivity. Such security is what the Johannine Jesus teaches Nicodemus: "The wind blows where it chooses, and you hear the sound of it, but you do not know where it comes from or where it goes. So it is with everyone who is born of the Spirit" (John 3:8). That verse could be translated as the spirit (or breath) blows where it chooses. What is born of Spirit is spirit; what is born of wind is wind! In other words, the Spirit appears to spirit invisibly! You do not know from where it comes or to where it goes, even though you experience it in some tangible way. Hearing the Spirit is like listening to the wind rattle wind chimes; you hear the music but you do not see the musician.

Meditation/Journal: What images other than wind, spirit, and breath can you identify for the Spirit?

Psalm Response: "O God! Your way is holy! / No god is great like God! / You're the God who makes things happen; / you showed everyone what you can do— / From Whirlwind came your thundering voice, / Lightning exposed the world, / Earth reeled and rocked. / You strode right through Ocean, / walked straight through roaring Ocean, / but nobody saw you come or go." (Ps 77:13–14, 18–19)

Spirit of Wisdom

Scripture: ". . . I prayed, and understanding was given me; / I called on God, and the spirit of wisdom came to me." (Wis 7:7)

Reflection: Biblically, the HB (OT) book of Deuteronomy is the first to mention the spirit of wisdom. Joshua, son of Nun, "was full of the spirit of wisdom" (Deut 34:9), according to the deuteronomist historian. When describing a new Davidic king, the prophet Isaiah states, "The spirit of the LORD shall rest on him, the spirit of wisdom" (Isa 11:2). However, it is not until the OT (A) book of Wisdom that the idea of the spirit of wisdom is fully developed. In the above verse, the author of the book writes in the name of King Solomon, recalling the famous episode in the HB (OT) First

Book of Kings (3:9) where the king prayed for wisdom to govern his people. The unknown author of the book of Wisdom recalls that episode to demonstrate that wisdom has a divine origin; wisdom was an extraordinary gift to Solomon from God; the spirit of wisdom was not merely the gift of intelligence, but a supernatural insight or spiritual gift. In the same chapter of the book of Wisdom, the author continues his lengthy reflection on the spirit of wisdom by placing his words on the lips of Solomon: ". . . [W]isdom, the fashioner of all things, taught me. / There is in her a spirit that is intelligent, holy, / unique, manifold, subtle, / mobile, clear, unpolluted, / distinct, invulnerable, loving the good, keen, / irresistible, beneficent, humane, / steadfast, sure, free from anxiety, / all-powerful, overseeing all, / and penetrating through all spirits / that are intelligent, pure, and altogether subtle. / For wisdom is more mobile than any motion; / because of her pureness she pervades and penetrates all things. / For she is a breath of the power of God, / and a pure emanation of the glory of the Almighty . . . . / For she is a reflection of eternal light, / a spotless mirror of the working of God, / and an image of his goodness. / Although she is but one, she can do all things, / and while remaining in herself, she renews all things; / in every generation she passes into holy souls / and makes them friends of God, and prophets; / for God loves nothing so much as the person who lives with wisdom" (Wis 7:23–28).

The author describes the spirit of wisdom with twenty-one attributes in three sets of seven. Seven represents divine perfection; three represents God (not Trinity). The spirit of wisdom possesses a rational nature (intelligent), and it is like God (holy), penetrating everything. In other words, "the spirit of the Lord has filled the world / and . . . holds all things together . . ." (Wis 1:7). Being a "kindly spirit" (Wis 1:6), it is also immaterial, omnipresent, and omnipotent, like God; in fact the author understand the spirit of wisdom and God to be identical. The spirit of wisdom comes forth from God like breath, like light; look over the shoulder of the spirit of wisdom into a mirror and see the image (reflection) of God. The Spirit of wisdom connects to human spirits, making them God's friends and prophets. Even though God's love is unearned and undeserved, he delights in people who love wisdom. To reject the spirit of wisdom is to reject God's love. Thus, the author of the OT (A) book of Wisdom presents Solomon asking God, "Who has learned your counsel, / unless you have given wisdom / and sent your holy spirit from on high?" (Wis 9:17) Solomon's words echo the spirit of wisdom's description as "a holy and disciplined spirit" (Wis 1:5). In the

CB (NT) letter to the Ephesians, the author prays that God will give his readers "a spirit of wisdom" as they come to know him (Eph 1:17).

Meditation/Journal: What attribute of the spirit of wisdom got most of your attention? As you reflect upon that attribute, in what ways do you find it within yourself?

Prayer Response: ". . . When I heard of the solid trust you have in the Master Jesus and your outpouring of love to all the followers of Jesus, I couldn't stop thanking God for you—every time I prayed, I'd think of you and give thanks. But I do more than thank. I ask—ask the God of our Master, Jesus Christ, the God of glory—to make you intelligent and discerning in knowing him personally, your eyes focused and clear, so that you can see exactly what it is he is calling you to do, grasp the immensity of his glorious way of life he has for his followers, oh, the utter extravagance of his work in us who trust him—endless energy, boundless strength!" (Eph 1:15–19)

Worship in Spirit

Scripture: Jesus said to the Samaritan woman at Jacob's well: ". . . [T]he hour is coming, and is now here, when the true worshipers will worship the Father in spirit and truth, for the Father seeks such as these to worship him. God is spirit, and those who worship him must worship in spirit and truth." (John 4:23–24)

Reflection: The above Scripture passage is taken from the lengthy story of Jesus at Jacob's well and his dialogue with a Samaritan woman in the CB (NT) Gospel of John (4:1–42). The Samaritan woman asks Jesus where was the best place to worship God; Samaritans worshiped on Mount Gerizim, but Jews worshiped in Jerusalem on Mount Moriah (Temple Mount). The Johannine Jesus states that his hour is coming—in the future of the narrative—but has already come for the post-resurrection, Johannine congregation (school), when the place for worship no longer matters. The Johannine Jesus denies true worship both to Samaritan and Jews, since they think of God as being connected with a holy place (mount, temple). According to Jesus, true worship of the Father occurs through Spirit and truth. In other words, genuine worship consists of human spirit being connected to the Spirit, which cannot be located. Truth is a reality of God. Thus, because God is Spirit, worshipers must worship in spirit and truth; in other words, they must worship in God. In so doing, worshipers transcend the earthly and experience the gift of the Spirit. Mount Gerizim and Mount Moriah are replaced by Jesus and his word, which, in turn, become the gift of the Spirit to believers.

Similarly, in his letter to the Philippians, Paul reminds his readers that they "worship in the Spirit of God" (Phil 3:3). They serve and minister to God, as a people devoted to God. In his letter, Paul reminds them that they worship in the Spirit of God; in other words, their worship is a gift. Worshiping in the Spirit of God is inclusive; as far as Paul is concerning, there is no longer a distinction between Jews and Gentiles. Christ Jesus has made it possible for all to be included; the Spirit of God connects to all human spirits—both Jews and Gentiles—and they worship God as one. All are God's people, worshiping him in and through his Spirit.

Meditation/Journal: In what place do you worship God? How do you respond to the Johannine Jesus who declares that place is not important? When have you experienced worship in Spirit and truth?

Psalm Response: "Train me, GOD, to walk straight; / then I'll follow your true path. / Put me together, one heart and mind; / then, undivided, I'll worship in joyful fear. / From the bottom of my heart I thank you, dear Lord; / I've never kept secret what you're up to. / You've always been great toward me—what love!" (Ps 86:11–13a)

X

Spirit of Xpist (Christ)

Scripture: "Anyone who does not have the Spirit of Christ does not belong to him." (Rom 8:9b)

Reflection: The *Xpist* in the above title is not a misprint; there is no English word *xpist*. *Xpist* is the English alphabet equivalent of the Greek word meaning anointed: *christ*. In Greek, ch is represented by x; r is represented by p, i is the same as i, s is the same as s, and t is the same as t. Thus, in the above passage, Paul tells the Romans that anyone not possessing the Spirit of *Xpist* (Christ = Anointed) does not belong to Christ (Anointed) Jesus.

Having the Spirit of Christ for Paul is a distinguishing mark of Christian identity drawn from Judaism. In the HB (OT) book of Exodus, God promises to dwell among the Israelites and be their God (Exod 29:45). In the CB (NT) Pauline view, God's promise has been expanded by the Spirit dwelling in the midst of the Christian community. In this charismatic understanding, the Spirit of Christ was thought to seize power and energize the community and its members.

The Spirit of Christ is also found in the CB (NT) First Letter of Peter. The author writes about salvation and the prophets' inquiry "about the person or time that the Spirit of Christ within them indicated. when it testified in advance to the sufferings destined for Christ and the subsequent glory" (1 Pet 1:11). According to the author, the prophets' searching and the Spirit's making manifest coincide, resulting in the prophetic announcement about Christ's passion, death, and resurrection, also an announcement from the Spirit. In other words, the author sees a continuity between prophets and gospel; both are inspired by the Spirit. Both confirm that suffering leads to glory. The prophetic message and the Christian gospel have the same source: the Spirit of the pre-existent (the Messiah of HB [OT] prophecy) Christ. The point the author is making is that there is continuity between prophetic message and Christian gospel, in terms of its heavenly origin (1 Pet 1:12): the Spirit of *Xpist* (Christ).

Meditation/Journal: Do you possess the Spirit of Christ? In what specific ways is it manifested?

Prayer Response: "What a God we have! And how fortunate we are to have him, this Father of our master Jesus! Because Jesus was raised from the dead, we've been given a brand-new life and have everything to live for, including a future in heaven—and the future starts now! God is keeping careful watch over us and the future. The Day is coming when you'll have it all—life healed and whole. The prophets who told us this was coming asked a lot of questions about this gift of life God was preparing. The Messiah's Spirit let them in on some of it—that the Messiah would experience suffering, followed by glory. They clamored to know who and when. All they were told was that they were serving you, you who by orders from heaven have now heard for yourselves—through the Holy Spirit—the Message of those prophecies fulfilled. Do you realize how fortunate you are?" (1 Pet 1:3–5, 10–12a)

ע

Spirit of ‌Yahweh (the LORD)

Scripture: "Who has directed the spirit of the LORD, / or as his counselor has instructed him?" (Isa 40:13)

Reflection: The phrase in the title above in parentheses—the LORD—with its all-capital letters for LORD is used commonly in Bibles where the name *Yahweh* occurs in Hebrew. Because the Divine Name, *YHWH* (Yahweh)—called the Tetragrammaton—was considered too sacred to pronounce and the Hebrew word *Adonai*, meaning Lord, was said instead of Yahweh, the tradition in printing English translations—stemming from translations from Hebrew into Greek (*Kyrios*) and Latin (*Dominus*)—became LORD (all capital letters). Most English translations of HB (OT) biblical texts replace YHWH (Yahweh) with LORD, as in the above Scripture text. In the Psalm Responses, taken from Eugene Peterson's *The Message*, in this book, the translator uses GOD (all capital letters) instead of LORD. The verse above comes from the opening chapter of what is commonly referred to as Deutero-Isaiah; biblical scholars have determined that chapters 40 through 55 were written by someone other than the person who wrote chapters 1 through 39; they call this unidentified author Second Isaiah, who wrote during the Babylonian exile and offered hope that Jerusalem would be restored by Yahweh (LORD). Unlike other deities, Israel's God depended on no one else for knowledge; his spirit was his active, life-giving power that came to rest on some (Isa 11:2). In the CB (NT) Acts of the Apostles, the Spirit of the Lord demonstrates his active, life-giving power by snatching Philip away from the Ethiopian eunuch, whom he had just baptized, who saw him no more (Acts 8:39).

Biblically, the spirit of Yahweh (the LORD), as we have seen in other entries in this book, came upon people (Judg 3:10; 11:29; 1 Sam 16:13; 2 Chr 20:14; Isa 61:1; Luke 4:18), took possession of people (Judg 6:34; 1 Sam 10:6), rushed on people (Judg 14:6, 19; 15:14), can pass by (1 Kgs 22:24; 2 Chr 18:23), can begin to stir someone (Judg 13:25), can speak through (2 Sam 23:2), can carry one (1 Kgs 18:12), can catch one up (2 Kgs 2:16), can rest on (Isa 11:2), can be given (Isa 63:14), can fall upon (Ezek 11:5), can be brought out (Ezek 37:1), can fill (Mic 38), can test (Acts 5:9), can give freedom (2 Cor 3:17), and can depart from a person (1 Sam 16:14). All totaled, the Spirit of Yahweh (the LORD) occurs twenty-seven times in biblical literature. No matter what it is described doing, it demonstrates God's active, life-giving power.

Meditation/Journal: When have you most recently experienced the Spirit of Yahweh (the LORD)? What active, life-giving power did you experience? Of the twenty-seven metaphors presented above, which one best describes your experience?

Prayer Response: "The Spirit of GOD, the Master, is on me / because GOD anointed me. / He sent me to preach good news to the poor, / heal the heartbroken, / Announce freedom to all captives, / pardon all prisoners. / GOD sent me to announce the year of his grace— / . . . and to comfort all who mourn." (Isa 61:1–2)

Z

Zeitgeist

Scripture: "Set your minds on things that are above, not on things that are on earth, for you have died, and your life is hidden with Christ in God. When Christ who is your life is revealed, then you also will be revealed with him in glory." (Col 3:2–4)

Reflection: While the German word *zeitgeist*—formed from *zeit*, meaning *time*, and *geist*, meaning *spirit*—does not occur in the above Scripture passage, the pericope from the CB (NT) letter to the Colossians captures the basic idea of *zeitgeist*, the general intellectual, moral, and culture climate of an era. According to the unknown author of Colossians, his readers should not conform to the climate in which they were living in the second century CE. Readers are told to set their minds on things above; living in the three-storied universe, things above refer to God, who lives on the third story. Reader are told not to set their minds on things on earth, the second story. The reason they should not conform to the *zeitgeist* is because they died in the baptismal pool and they were raised to new life that is hidden with Christ in God. Believers have not been removed from earth, they mold everyday life according to the intellectual, moral, and cultural climate of the world above, where God lives. Their old lives have been set aside through death in baptism; their new life has been quickened by God's Spirit, which makes it hidden with Christ in God. One day, however, what is secretly present will become manifest, when Christ returns in glory from the world above to the earth. The life of the Spirit that was begun in baptism will then reach its fulfillment in unending glory. In other words, the author exhorts his readers to stay focused on the third story of the world and not to focus on the second story. Their concerns should not be the ordinary, self-centered, pursuits, but living a spiritual life, a life guided by God's Spirit in the hope of total spiritual fulfillment, when Christ returns to the earth in glory.

Besides the German *geist* for the English *spirit*, there is also the French *esprit*, the Spanish *espiritu*, and the Portuguese *espirito*, all formed from the Latin *spiritus*. We have already explored the Greek *pneuma*, and the Hebrew *ruah*, which becomes the basis for the Arabic *ruh*. There is also the Russian *dukh*. All words attempt to capture the meaning of the non-capturable divine Spirit.

Meditation/Journal: After some meditation, where do you discover your focus to be: the world above or the world below? How would you characterize the *zeitgeist* of each? What is your favorite word for spirit? Why?

Psalm Response: "Get insurance with GOD and do a good deed, / settle down and stick to your last. / Keep company with GOD, / get in on the best. / Open up before GOD, keep nothing back; / he'll do whatever needs to be done; / He'll validate your life in the clear light of day / and stamp you with approval at high noon. / Quiet down before GOD, / be prayerful before him." (Ps 37:3–7a)

Bibliography

O'Day, Gail R., and David Petersen, eds. *The Access Bible: New Revised Standard Version with the Apocryphal/Deuterocanonical Books, Updated Edition.* New York: Oxford University Press, 2011.

Peterson, Eugene H., and William Griffin, trans. *The Message: Catholic/Ecumenical Edition, The Bible in Contemporary Language.* Chicago, IL; ACTA, 2013.

Recent Books by Mark G. Boyer

Published by Wipf & Stock

Nature Spirituality: Praying with Wind, Water, Earth, Fire

A Spirituality of Ageing

Weekday Saints: Reflections on Their Scriptures

Human Wholeness: A Spirituality of Relationship

A Simple Systematic Mariology

Praying Your Way through Luke's Gospel and the Acts of the Apostles

An Abecedarian of Animal Spirit Guides: Spiritual Growth through Reflections on Creatures

Overcome with Paschal Joy: Chanting through Lent and Easter—Daily Reflections with Familiar Hymns

Taking Leave of Your Home: Moving in the Peace of Christ

An Abecedarian of Sacred Trees: Spiritual Growth through Reflections on Woody Plants

Divine Presence: Elements of Biblical Theophanies

Fruit of the Vine: A Biblical Spirituality of Wine

Names for Jesus: Reflections for Advent and Christmas

Talk to God and Listen to the Casual Reply: Experiencing the Spirituality of John Denver

Christ Our Passover Has Been Sacrificed: A Guide through Paschal Mystery Spirituality—Mystical Theology in The Roman Missal

Rosary Primer: The Prayers, The Mysteries, and the New Testament

From Contemplation to Action: The Spiritual Process of Divine Discernment Using Elijah and Elisha as Models

Love Addict

All Things Mary: Honoring the Mother of God—An Anthology of Marian Reflections

Shhh! The Sound of Sheer Silence: A Biblical Spirituality that Transforms

RECENT BOOKS BY MARK G. BOYER

What is Born of the Spirit is Spirit: A Biblical Spirituality of Spirit

Very Short Reflections—for Advent and Christmas, Lent and Easter, Ordinary Time, and Saints—through the Liturgical Year

Living Parables: Today's Versions

My Life of Ministry, Writing, Teaching, and Traveling: The Autobiography of an Old Mines Missionary

300 Years of the French in Old Mines: A Narrative History of the Oldest Village in Missouri

Journey into God: Spiritual Reflections for Travelers

Monthly Entries for the Spiritual but not Religious through the Year: Texts, Reflections, Journal/Meditations, and Prayers for the Spiritual but not Religious

The Shelbydog Chronicles by Shelby Cole as Recorded by Mark G. Boyer: A Novel

Four Catholic Pioneers in Missouri: Lamarque, Kenrick, Fox, and Hogan: Irish Missionaries and Their Supporter

Smothered with Inexhaustible Mercy: An Anthology of Poems

Spirituality for the Solitary: A Handbook for Those Who Live Alone

Seasons of Biblical Spirituality: Spring, Summer, Autumn, Winter

Biblical Names for God: An Abecedarian Anthology of Spiritual Reflections for Anytime

More Shelbydog Chronicles: Reflections on a Dog's Life by Her Friend, Knowing Your Pet

His Mercy Endures Forever: Biblical Reflections on Divine Mercy for Anytime

The Roman Catholic Lectionary and the Bible: Analysis, Conclusions, Suggested Alternatives